*Virginia History
in
Documents
1621-1788*

Virginia History
in
Documents
1621-1788

by

WILLIAM H. GAINES, JR.

Virginia State Library
Richmond, Virginia
1974

Published under authority of the
Library Board of Virginia

COPYRIGHT © THE VIRGINIA STATE LIBRARY, 1974
ISBN: 0-88490-000-2
Library of Congress Catalog Card Number: 73-94133
Printed in the United States of America

Contents

Preface

The documents reproduced in this set of facsimiles have been selected because of their importance in the early constitutional history of Virginia. Represented here are the writings of such famous men as Nathaniel Bacon, Patrick Henry, Edmund Pendleton, George Mason, James Madison, and Thomas Jefferson, as well as those of some lesser known figures. Particular items throw light on the feelings and thoughts of Virginians about such events as the establishment of the General Assembly, the movement for independence, and the formation of the American Union. Some documents have primarily a local interest, while others have influenced events and developments far beyond Virginia's borders. A reading of them reveals views and attitudes toward such issues as religious freedom, the role of government in human affairs, and the right of revolution.

These documents cover the period from the founding of the Virginia colony to the ratification of the Constitution of the United States. A second set of documents will deal with the state's history as part of the federal Union.

Virginia History in Documents
1621-1788

Introduction

The Documents: Three Basic Themes

Each item in this group of Virginia documents was produced by practical men dealing with practical situations rather than by philosophers setting forth theoretical ideas. The authors did not pretend to be absolutely original thinkers, and in many cases they borrowed freely from the writings of other men. Their ideas were not unusual in either Europe or America: men in other colonies and states held ideas similar to those set forth in the documents reproduced here. The Virginians who drew up these papers were responding to particular challenges and were attempting to offset particular perils. The ideas they expressed should be judged in the light of the circumstances which brought them into being. Their authors, however, were often motivated by ideals that went beyond the immediate needs of their time, and they were inspired by a larger vision than that of temporary political advantage. Their expression of fundamental principles transcended their immediate political context to such an extent that the ideas they developed still have relevance today.

While the documents reproduced here cover a wide range of time and subject matter, they may be considered in the light of three predominant themes: (1) the development and maintenance of self-government, (2) the struggle for individual rights, and (3) participation in the common cause of national unity. In the course of Virginia history, the themes have sometimes overlapped and complemented each other; at other times, one theme has been in conflict with another.

I: *The Idea of Self-Government*

The people of Virginia have cherished self-government almost from the beginning of their history, and they have striven repeatedly to preserve the freedom of managing their own internal affairs. As Englishmen, the first settlers were familiar with the idea of a legislature composed of representatives from every part of the realm. For more than two centuries the House of Commons, the lower chamber of Parliament, had been an essential and influential part of the governmental system. The London Company, which controlled Virginia affairs from the founding of the colony in 1607 to the assertion of royal control in 1624, was also a representative body.

Virginians began making their own laws with the establishment of the "General Assembly," which met for the first time at Jamestown in the summer of 1619. The purposes of the Assembly were set forth in the "Ordinance and Constitution" (Document #1), issued by the London Company in 1621. The officers of the company, chosen by the stockholders and responsible to them, instituted the idea of a representative legislature in the colony in order "to settle such a forme of government as may be to the greatest benefit and comfort of the people." All matters coming before the Assembly, whose members were to be elected from the different settlements along the James, were to be "decided, determined & ordered by the greater part of the voices then present."

During the seventeenth century the Virginia Assembly grew in size and in importance. The House of Burgesses, as the lower chamber came to be called, began to meet separately from the Council, just as the English House of Commons sat apart from the House of Lords. Its members thus began to think and act in an increasingly independent manner and came to consider themselves as spokesmen for the people they represented and as the proper guardians of their liberties.

The desire of Virginians to preserve the independence of their local assembly inspired the colony's resistance to royal authority.

Colonial Virginians were particularly vigilant where taxation was concerned, as they demonstrated in their response to the Stamp Act, a revenue measure passed by Parliament in 1765. The Assembly adopted resolutions of protest drafted by Patrick Henry (Document #3), in which they condemned the measure as an interference with their powers of legislation: the power to tax themselves, so the author of the resolutions asserted, was "the

The English House of Commons, shown here as it appeared in 1651, was the model for the Virginia House of Burgesses.

distinguishing Characteristick of British freedom." The General Assembly possessed "the only and sole exclusive Right & Power to lay Taxes & impositions upon the Inhabitants of this Colony." Members of the House of Burgesses, so Henry declared, knew better than members of Parliament what taxes could be borne by Virginians. Since the burgesses were equally affected themselves by the taxes they levied and by the laws they passed, they were more competent to deal fairly with such matters than any official in London.

During the next few years, the House of Burgesses frequently protested against British policy. Several royal governors, among them Fauquier, Botetourt, and Dunmore, sought to discourage the zeal of the members by "dissolving" (that is, dismissing) the House. When the burgesses realized that they could not work effectively as long as they were part of a system that included unsympathetic governors, they began to meet and act independently. Their most important gathering came late in May, 1774, just after Dunmore dissolved the Assembly for its resolutions on the Boston Port Bill. On May 27, eighty-nine burgesses—acting on their own initiative—signed an "association," recommending that Virginia send delegates to the intercolonial assembly that became the First Continental Congress. Three days later, on May 30, twenty-five burgesses still present in Williamsburg summoned their absent colleagues to come together as a convention in August to take up matters of joint concern (Document #4). They did so knowing that Dunmore would not recall the Assembly, and they expected to deal with matters which ordinarily would have been forbidden to them.

Virginians further demonstrated their desire to preserve their local freedom in the very act of declaring their separation from the British Empire. In the Resolutions for Independence, passed on May 15, 1776 (Document #5), the Virginia convention urged the state's delegates in the Continental Congress to work for an intercolonial plan of union, but the members of the convention were careful to include the stipulation that "the internal concerns of each colony . . . be left to the respective colonial legislatures." To carry out their new independence, Virginians framed a written constitution (Document #7), the first such instrument of government ever to be adopted by a self-governing commonwealth. By their action they were assuming the status of a sovereign state, responsible to no higher political authority.

For the next twelve years Virginians enjoyed almost complete self-government and became more thoroughly convinced of the benefits of autonomy. In 1788 when the state surrendered part of her sovereignty in order to form "a more perfect union," she did so with distinct reservations. The Virginia convention which ratified the new federal Constitution that year (Document #10) gave notice that the commonwealth would resume her sovereignty if the federal government ever "perverted" the powers granted it by the Constitution. Most of the other states made similar reservations at the time of ratification.

II: *The Idea of Individual Rights*

Next to their regard for self-government, Virginians have cherished the rights of the individual citizen. One may trace the development of their concern through three major phases, each of which is marked by a particular stage in the political development of the state. Virginians have appealed in succession to English concepts of liberty, then to the more universal doctrine of natural rights, and finally to the written guarantees of the American Constitution. The first stage lasted throughout the colonial era; the second began when the decision for independence was made and continued throughout the War of the Revolution and its immediate aftermath; the last came into existence with the adoption of the present federal system.

Virginians of the mid-eighteenth century contended that as Englishmen they possessed the same rights and liberties as Englishmen at home, and that they had enjoyed these rights since the colony was first established. King James I in his charter to the London Company of 1606 had guaranteed that all who settled in the new world, and their descendants, would have the same "liberties, franchises, and immunities . . . as if they had been abiding and borne [*sic*] within this our realm of England." Subsequent charters in 1609 and in 1612 reaffirmed these guarantees, and the creation of the General Assembly in 1619 provided an instrument for the protection of such rights.

Early English liberties were primarily legal and procedural in their nature and were meant to secure the person and property (real and personal) of the individual against arbitrary rulers. These rights had their roots in the late Middle Ages and rested upon the English common law. During the seventeenth and early eighteenth centuries, the concept of English liberty had been strengthened and reaffirmed, particularly after the struggle between Parliament and the crown culminated in the "Glorious Revolution" of 1688. By that event England—and indirectly her American colonies— escaped the threat of rule by an absolute monarch and became a constitutional kingdom deriving its power from Parliament.

By the end of the colonial period it was generally recognized— at least in theory—that no Englishman could be subjected to arbitrary arrest or imprisonment, and that his goods could not be taken from him except by legal process: it came to be said that an Englishman's house was his "castle," secure against all unauthorized entry. The "free-born Briton," furthermore, could not be subjected to martial law or taxed without the consent of his representatives in Parliament.

It is true that these rights were not always scrupulously observed, particularly when they involved the poor and the propertyless. It is also true that English liberties did not extend to such personal rights, later considered fundamental, as those involving freedom of expression. As James Madison put it in 1789, the English constitution simply did not protect freedom of religion or freedom of the press, "those choicest privileges of the people." Nonetheless, the ordinary Englishman by the late eighteenth century was freer in his person and his property than his counterpart in any other European state of the day, with the possible exception of Holland. Englishmen on both sides of the Atlantic prided themselves on their freedom, and they strove whenever necessary to preserve and maintain it.

Colonial appeals to English concepts of liberty were logical only so long as the colonists still remained loyal to the English connection. By the spring of 1776, however, Virginians were in arms against British troops, and Virginia was on the verge of declaring independence. Because they no longer had any justification for claiming the protection of English liberties, Virginians began their existence as members of an independent commonwealth by appealing to rights that appertained to them, not as subjects of an English king, but as members of the human race. The patriots of 1776 took up the ancient doctrine of natural rights—a doctrine that was universal in its implications.

The concept of natural rights was, of course, not a new one. It was inherent in the doctrine of natural law which had been first expounded by the Stoic philosophers in the classical age and later adapted to Christian doctrine by the great medieval theologians.

The English political philosopher John Locke proclaimed that every man had a right to life, liberty, and property. His teachings inspired many of Virginia's revolutionary leaders.

Support for the idea could also be found in the teachings of Jesus, who had emphasized the sanctity and dignity of the individual soul; in the writings of the Protestant reformers; and, more recently, in the works of the secular authors of the Enlightenment. John Locke (1632-1704), the seventeenth-century English philosopher, had declared that every man possessed "indefeasible" rights to be secure in his life, his liberty, and his property: no government could infringe those rights except by process of law. Writers as different in outlook as the poet John Milton (1608-1674) and the lawyer and jurist Sir William Blackstone (1723-1780) supported the same general concept. The teachings of such men were well known to colonists of the revolutionary generation; and Virginians drew freely on their ideas and expanded upon them.

The Virginia Declaration of Rights (Document #6) was a particularly succinct statement of the doctrine. It held that men were "created equally free and independent" and were therefore endowed with "certain inherent natural rights." Among these were "the enjoyment of life and liberty, with the means of acquiring and possessing property, and pursuing and obtaining happiness and safety." These rights came from God, and were not privileges to be bestowed—or withdrawn—by any earthly ruler.

In taking up the doctrine of natural rights, the Virginians still retained a basically English view of individual liberty. Of the rights specified in the declaration, many were those that the colonists had been claiming for generations. Among these was the assertion that men could not be "taxed or deprived of their property for public uses without their own Consent or that of their Representatives . . . nor bound by any Law to which, they have not, in like Manner, assented, for the public Good." The declaration also contended that accused persons were entitled to trial by jury and to other legal safeguards that were part of the English heritage. Rights earlier claimed on the basis of English citizenship were made universal and applicable to everybody.

The natural rights doctrine was broader and more inclusive than the concept it replaced, and the Declaration of Rights reflected the

Virginia legislators met in this Richmond warehouse from 1780 to 1788. Here they debated and passed both the Resolutions for the Cession of Lands and the Bill for Religious Freedom.

wider outlook. That document specifically classified freedom of the press and "the free exercise of Religion" as natural rights. Each of these freedoms had been asserted earlier in England and in America—one thinks of John Milton and William Penn and Peter Zenger—but the declaration gave each a force and sanction that it had not previously possessed. The "free exercise of religion" was given special emphasis almost ten years later when the Virginia General Assembly passed Thomas Jefferson's Bill for Religious Freedom (Document #8), with its firm assertion that freedom of worship was "one of the natural rights of mankind."

There were significant differences between traditional English liberties and the theory of natural rights. The former, largely legal and judicial in nature, were designed for the protection of person and property; the latter were much broader and covered the right of opinion. English liberties, even as they had developed by the late eighteenth century, pertained to *subjects* owing obedience and allegiance to a monarch; natural rights, on the other hand, were to be enjoyed by *citizens* able and qualified to participate in the conduct of their own government.

Within a little more than a decade after independence, when Virginians decided to join with other states to form "a more perfect union," they saw that firm written guarantees would be necessary to protect individual rights under the new central government. They remembered that Parliament itself had not always respected the liberties of Englishmen, and they feared that an American Congress (particularly with the extensive powers granted it under the proposed federal Constitution) might be tempted at some future time to curtail or restrict the individual rights of Virginians and other Americans.

Men of the post-revolutionary generation sought to avoid that danger by writing guarantees into the nation's fundamental law and thus put the rights of the individual beyond the reach of either the executive or the legislative power. The Virginia convention which ratified the federal Constitution in 1788 (Document #10) specifically declared that "liberty of conscience and of the press" were "essential rights" which could never be abolished or changed "by any authority of the United States." The same body also urged the adoption of amendments specifically protecting individual rights: these additions to the Constitution became the Bill of Rights. After the adoption of the first ten amendments, Virginians—and other Americans—could resort to constitutional protection for the maintenance of their "natural" rights.

III: *The Idea of the "Common Cause"*

While Virginians have often seemed preoccupied with their local concerns and with the preservation of their local liberties,

The Second Continental Congress, in which Virginia and her sister states worked together for the "common cause," met in the Pennsylvania State House, now called Independence Hall.

they have also shown a capacity to look beyond their own borders and to work for the "common cause" of American Union. Accordingly, they have frequently played a positive role in the creation and the preservation of the Union. Even before declaring for independence, the Old Dominion took the lead in proposing a common action by the colonies as a means of producing more effective resistance to British power. In May, 1774, a group of burgesses, meeting unofficially, endorsed a suggestion that Virginia should "concur with the other Colonies in such measures as shall be judged most effectual for the Preservation of the Common Rights and Liberty of British America" (Document #4). As a result of their action, the first of Virginia's revolutionary conventions assembled two months later. It was this body that chose the delegates who represented the colony in the First Continental Congress, which gathered at Philadelphia that September.

Two years later Virginia took a further step and recommended a formal union of the colonies, which by that time were in open revolt against Great Britain. In the Resolutions for Independence, adopted on May 15, 1776 (Document #5), the revolutionary convention instructed Virginia's delegates in the Second Continental Congress to support "whatever measures may be thought proper and necessary" for "a confederation of the colonies." This proposal led to the drafting, and eventually to the adoption, of the first national constitution, the Articles of Confederation.

Virginia further contributed to the "common cause" in 1781 when she ceded to the central government her claims to lands she held north of the Ohio River (Document #9). The General Assembly, in making the decision to sacrifice that territory, did so because the members were convinced that "the happiness, strength and safety" of the American Union was at stake. "The good of their country" and "the benefit of the United States," the Assembly declared, took precedence over "every object of smaller importance."

The Old Dominion made another vital contribution to American unity in the role she played in the drafting and the adoption of the federal Constitution. In 1786 the General Assembly passed a law appointing delegates to a convention in Philadelphia "for the purpose of revising" the Articles of Confederation. As matters turned out, the convention at Philadelphia produced the present federal Constitution. In 1788 a state convention, meeting at Richmond, voted to adopt the new form of government (Document #10). When faced with a choice between maintaining their own freedom of action and meeting the threat to "the common cause" of America, the people of the commonwealth gave up part of their cherished sovereignty to make possible "a more perfect union."

*   *   *   *

Self-government, human rights, the Union—these three themes run through Virginia's history as colony and as commonwealth. Sometimes one theme, sometimes another, has been in the ascendant. Through the interaction of these themes one may trace the state's early constitutional development.

An Ordinance and Constitution for a Council and Assembly in Virginia

July 24, 1621

DOCUMENT NO. 1

In January, 1619, a ship sailed from London bound for America. Among the passengers were Sir George Yeardley, the new governor of the Virginia colony, and his wife Temperance. With him Yeardley carried detailed instructions from his superiors in the London Company, which had directed the affairs of the colony since 1609. His instructions were designed to improve economic conditions in Virginia, still struggling for existence twelve years after its founding in 1607, and to establish "a laudable form of government" there.

Yeardley was well-equipped to carry out the new policy, for he was thoroughly familiar with Virginia and with its problems. He had first arrived at Jamestown in 1610, after a period of military service in the Netherlands, and had lived in the colony for about eight years, during which time he had been occupied in a military capacity. He had also served as governor from April, 1616, to May, 1617, and had carried out his duties with both firmness and mildness. He had returned to England by early 1618; a few months later the London Company commissioned him as governor and captain general of Virginia. King James then knighted him—much to the pleasure of his wife who, it was said, thoroughly enjoyed being known as Lady Yeardley.

During the long voyage back across the stormy Atlantic, Yeardley must have studied the two commissions which the London Company had given him. One of the two documents—both of

13

which had been adopted by the company on November 18, 1618—provided for a new landholding system in Virginia; the other (which is reproduced here) laid the basis for an experiment in self-government in a community that had lived under martial law for twelve years. It called for the establishment of a Council of State and a General Assembly and so led to the founding of the first representative legislature in the New World.

The commission expressed the company's desire that the new government might alleviate "all injustice, grievance and oppression" and provide for "the greatest benefit and comfort of the people." Eager to turn a handsome profit, the officers of the company also expressed the hope that the new government would promote the "strength, stability and prosperity" of the colony.

The commission provided that the Council of State was to consist of the governor and other principal officers of the colony and about twelve of the more substantial settlers. The councillors were directed to assist the governor "with their care, advice, and circumspection" in all matters.

Although the Council was similar to the advisory groups that had aided previous governors, the General Assembly represented a real innovation for the colony. This body was to be "more general" (that is, more representative) than the Council of State and was to consist of the Council and "two burgesses out of every towne, hundred, and other particular plantation." The burgesses (or representatives) were to be elected by the inhabitants of the various settlements and were to meet annually at the call of the governor. All matters coming before the Assembly were to be "decided, determined and ordered by the greater part of the voices then present," but the governor was always to have the power of overruling its decisions. Under the terms of the commission, the Assembly was to "have free power to treat, consult and conclude" on all matters concerning the welfare of the colony, and "to make, ordain, and enact such general laws & orders for the behoof of the said Colony and the good government thereof." All laws passed by the Assembly had to conform to the laws and customs "used in the realm of England," and had to be approved by the London Company before becoming effective.

The idea of a representative legislature was a familiar one to seventeenth-century Englishmen. There were models for such a body, both in the House of Commons, where the shires and towns of England sent representatives to Parliament, and in the organization of the London Company itself. Since 1612 the affairs of the company had been conducted in four quarterly "courts," or general meetings, in which all shareholders were able to participate. Voting was by "erection of hands": every member present had an equal voice with every other, no matter how many shares of company stock he owned. In establishing a General Assembly for Virginia, the London Company was therefore extending to the colony its own form of internal government.

Soon after Yeardley landed at Jamestown in April, 1619, he called on the colonists to choose their representatives for the forthcoming Assembly. That spring Virginians up and down the James took part in the first elections ever held in the New World. The twenty-two men they chose—representing the four "great boroughs" of James City, Charles City, Henricus, and Kiccotawn (later Elizabeth City), and seven smaller communities—met with Yeardley and his Council on July 30, 1619, in the church at Jamestown. The session opened with a prayer for divine guidance, after which the Speaker "explained the occasion of their meeting" and read the commission creating the Assembly.

That first Assembly remained in session for only six days and transacted mostly routine business. It set a precedent, however, and the General Assembly continued to meet periodically, even after 1624 when the crown took over direct control of the colony from the company. Legislative government in the United States thus owes its beginnings to a profit-seeking English trading company, whose members were inspired in 1618 "to lay a foundation whereon a flourishing state might in process of time by the blessing of Almighty God be raised." The General Assembly of Virginia, a direct descendant of that meeting in the Jamestown church, deserves its reputation as the oldest representative body in the New World.

*   *   *   *

No manuscript copy of the original commission which Yeardley took to Virginia in 1619 has survived. The London Company reissued the document two years later when it sent out instructions for the guidance of Sir Francis Wyatt, Yeardley's successor. This version of the document, dated July 24, 1621, is entitled "An Ordinance and Constitution for a Council and Assembly in Virginia." Except for the substitution of several names to reflect changes in the makeup of the Council, it is believed to be a true copy of Yeardley's commission. The original of the 1621 copy of the ordinance may be found in the Manuscript Records of the Virginia Company in the Manuscript Division, Library of Congress, Washington, D.C. It is reproduced with the permission of that depository.

The Declaration of the People Against Sir William Berkeley

July 30, 1676

DOCUMENT No. 2

On July 29, 1676, young Nathaniel Bacon, proclaiming himself "Generall by the Consent of the People," led a party of armed Virginians to a settlement called Middle Plantation, about six miles north of Jamestown. The next day Bacon—who had been at odds with the royal governor, Sir William Berkeley, since spring—took the final and irrevocable step of open rebellion against the king's representative. On behalf of "the People in all the Counties in Virginia," he issued a proclamation condemning Berkeley for his misgovernment of the colony. Bacon's Rebellion, one of the most dramatic events in the history of the colony, had entered its final and crucial stage.

Opposition to Berkeley's Indian policy, particularly his failure to provide for the defense of the frontier counties, sparked the rebellion, but many colonists also had deep-seated political grievances. Sir William had ruled as governor without interruption for sixteen years; by 1676 he and his supporters, through a monopoly of offices, controlled the government of the colony at every level. Most settlers felt themselves cut off from any meaningful share in the political process.

Bacon, who had arrived in Virginia two years earlier, was drawn into the opposition movement early in 1676, when Indians killed the overseer of his James River plantation. The young planter, because of his family connections, was a member of Berkeley's Council. Although he was identified with the colony's political leadership, he turned his back on the established government and in defiance of Berkeley's wishes led an expedition against the natives to punish them for their attack. His act of insubordination was followed by a series of confrontations with Berkeley that reached a climax in mid-July, when the governor went into Gloucester County to raise a force against his young rival.

Bacon was on his way back to the frontier to resume the Indian campaign when he learned of Berkeley's move. He and his men immediately returned to the Tidewater to confront the government forces. He came ready to do battle, even though he was putting himself and his followers in open rebellion. His army of about five hundred men arrived at Middle Plantation on July 29, and the following day he issued "The Declaration of the People." In that document Bacon justified his defiance of the authorities by attacking Berkeley. The rebel leader was not seeking an independent Virginia: he was careful, indeed, to make several loyal references to the king so it would appear that Berkeley was the villain in the case—that the governor and his followers were "Traytors to the King and Countrie." The basic assumption in the declaration was that "the People" were justified in their resistance to Berkeley, since such resistance provided the only remedy for the wrongs they suffered.

The governor, so Bacon charged in his declaration, had "raised unjust taxes upon . . . the Commonalitie"; he had, "during the Long time of his Government," neglected measures for promoting the colony's welfare, "either by Fortifications, Towns, or Trade." He had appointed "Scandalous and ignorant Favourites" to public positions and had sought to monopolize the fur trade with the Indians. By failing to take proper military action against them, the old man had "protected, favoured, and Emboldened the Indians." Finally, Berkeley's action in raising troops to oppose Bacon had brought "Civill Warr and Destruction" upon the people of Virginia.

The declaration was aimed not only at the governor but also at nineteen of his "wicked and Pernicious Councellors." Bacon ordered that Berkeley, "with all the Persons in this List, be forth-

Several weeks after Nathaniel Bacon issued his Declaration of the People, he and his men captured and burned Jamestown.

with delivered upp, or Surrender Themselves within foure dayes." All other persons who helped the governor in any way were to be dealt with as "Traytors to the People." Bacon issued his orders "in the Name of the People, in all the Counties in Virginia," and signed his proclamation as "Generall by the Consent of the People." While it is difficult to determine the extent of Bacons' actual support among "the People," it is likely that a majority of them were, at this time, sympathetic to his cause.

For all of its fiery rhetoric, the declaration produced few tangible results. The rebels did capture Jamestown—the capital of the colony—and then burned the town. The governor fled to the Eastern Shore, and for a few weeks Bacon was the unchallenged master of the entire colony west of Chesapeake Bay. A month later the dynamic young leader fell suddenly ill and died, the rebellion collapsed, and Berkeley reasserted his authority with harsh brutality. Virginia remained under royal control for a century more, and Bacon's name was almost forgotten. His memory was revived only after Virginians had won their independence from Great Britain, and his present reputation as Virginia's first popular champion is of comparatively recent origin.

The significance of Bacon's declaration lies in its claim to speak for "the People" and for "the Commons of Virginia." The belief, implied rather than stated directly, that "the People" are the ultimate source of governmental power is the principal justification for democracy itself.

*   *   *   *

The facsimile of the Declaration of the People is reproduced from the manuscript copy in the Blathwayt Papers in the collections of The Colonial Williamsburg Foundation, Williamsburg, Virginia, and it is copied with the permission of that institution.

Patrick Henry's Resolutions Against the Stamp Act

May 30, 1765

Parliament passed the Stamp Act on March 22, 1765, and late the following May a copy of the act "crept into" the Virginia House of Burgesses. Because that body, then in session at the capitol in Williamsburg, had concluded the major part of its business, most of the members had already left for their homes. Only 39 of the 113 burgesses were present on May 29 when Patrick Henry of Louisa County took the floor to propose that the House "consider the Steps necessary to be taken" in regard to the new law from London. An able lawyer, Henry had first taken his seat just nine days earlier. In his own words, he was "inexperienced, unacquainted with the Forms of the House, & the Members that composed it."

At the age of twenty-nine, Henry had already won a reputation as a popular champion because of his efforts in the Parson's Cause. In that case, involving the right of the Virginia Assembly to fix the salaries of clergymen, he had questioned the king's power to disallow (or veto) acts passed by the General Assembly. Now he rose to challenge the right of Parliament to tax the colonists directly. Since the older and more experienced members seemed "averse to opposition," the new burgess himself took the initiative, drew up a set of resolutions on the subject, and presented them to the House.

The Stamp Act was designed to raise revenue for the support of British garrisons in the trans-Allegheny West, recently conquered from France. The law required the colonists to use official stamps purchased from government agents on a wide variety of legal and business documents, newspapers, and other items. Parliament had insisted on passing the act, although the Virginia House of Burgesses and other colonial assemblies had earlier submitted petitions against it.

Henry's resolutions, which he wrote out on "a blank leaf of an old Law Book," denied the authority of Parliament to lay such a tax. "The first Adventurers and Settlers" of Virginia, he declared, had "brought with them and transmitted to their Posterity" the same rights and liberties that were enjoyed by the people of England. The charter of 1606, granted to the colony by James I, had guaranteed that the colonists were entitled to those rights "as if they had been abiding and born within the realm of England." The right of the people to tax themselves, either directly or "by Persons chosen by themselves to represent them," was one of the most vital of those "Priviledges, Liberties and Immunities." This right was "the distinguishing Characteristick of British Freedom." Representatives chosen by the people knew better than any outside authority "what Taxes the People are able to bear," and would be "equally affected by such Taxes themselves."

There was little in the statements summarized above (they may be read in the first four paragraphs of the facsimile) that was either new or startling. Most of these points had been raised in petitions submitted to the king and to Parliament by the Assembly the previous December, and some of Henry's language was almost identical to that used in the earlier documents. Henry, however, went much further than some of his colleagues were willing to go when he declared that the Virginia General Assembly had "the *only and sole exclusive* Right" to tax the people of the colony.

Henry's resolutions were debated in the House of Burgesses on May 30. In the course of the argument, which Thomas Jefferson later remembered as "most bloody" and which Henry himself recalled as "long and warm," the lawyer from Louisa delivered his famous speech comparing George III to Julius Caesar and

Charles I. Four of his resolutions passed by five votes, and a fifth—most likely the one claiming that the "sole exclusive **Right**" of taxation rested in the Assembly—prevailed by only one vote and was later rescinded. The official version, as recorded in the House journal, contained only the first four of the five resolutions that appear on Henry's copy.

The Virginia resolves against the Stamp Act preceded and inspired similar action in other colonies and led to the summoning of an intercolonial assembly. Meeting in New York City in October, the Stamp Act Congress (which was called at the suggestion of Massachusetts and to which, ironically enough, Virginia did not send representatives) adopted resolutions similar in tone and content to Henry's proposals. Meanwhile mob violence against the newly appointed stamp collectors had broken out in various towns throughout America. Some colonists adopted the less provocative step of refusing to import or use British goods. Largely because of this boycott, which directly affected British merchants selling

Stamps like these were required on legal documents, business papers, newspapers, and other articles.

goods to America, Parliament repealed the Stamp Act in March, 1766. At the same time, however, it affirmed its right to legislate for the colonies "in all cases whatsoever" and thus paved the way for future clashes.

Henry summed up his own opinion of his resolutions in the comment he wrote after the Revolution was over. By forming "the first Opposition" to British attempts to tax America, they had established the "great point of Resistance" to parliamentary policy. It was this resistance that "brought on the War which finally separated the two Countrys, and gave Independence to ours."

The resolutions were important, not only because they specifically upheld the right of the people to tax themselves, but also because they firmly asserted the broader right of representative self-government. Long after Virginians ceased to rest their claims to liberty on their rights as British subjects, they continued to defend local autonomy as "the distinguishing Characteristick" of American freedom.

*   *   *   *

The first draft of the resolutions was written out, as the author later recalled, on "a blank leaf of an old Law Book," and is now lost. The copy reproduced here is not in Henry's hand but in that of his colleague, John Fleming of Cumberland County. Henry had this copy in his possession by the end of the war, when he added the endorsement on the back. The copy was retained by Henry's family after his death at Red Hill, Charlotte County, in 1799, and is now in the possession of The Colonial Williamsburg Foundation, Williamsburg, Virginia. It is reproduced with their permission.

DOCUMENT NO. 4

On December 16, 1773, a crowd of patriots went aboard three English merchant ships in Boston harbor and tossed 342 chests of imported tea into the cold waters. The British government reacted swiftly and harshly to the latest display of colonial resistance. Early in 1774 Parliament passed a law closing the port of Boston until the tea was paid for.

The first news of the Boston Port Bill reached Williamsburg on May 19, 1774, where the Virginia House of Burgesses was in session. Five days later the members—moved to sympathy by the plight of their fellow Americans—passed a set of resolutions expressing their support of the Bostonians. To demonstrate their concern, they ordered that June 1, the date the Port Bill was to take effect, be observed in Virginia as a day of fasting and prayer. The resolution, so Thomas Jefferson related years later, was "cooked up" by a group of younger members including himself, but it was supported by all the other burgesses and was passed without opposition.

On May 26, two days after passage of the resolution, the royal governor, Lord Dunmore, summoned the burgesses to meet with him in the Council chamber. He had seen a copy of their resolutions and found them objectionable. He informed the burgesses that they were "dissolved" and that the Assembly was no longer in session. Undoubtedly he expected that they would quietly disperse and go home.

The Boston Tea Party, by provoking an angry retaliation from the British government, led to Virginia's call for a Continental Congress.

On this occasion, however, the burgesses refused to break up. Most of them immediately gathered at the Raleigh Tavern, a short walk from the capitol, to resume their deliberations. The next day, with nearly all the members of the "late House present," the stubborn Virginians drafted and adopted an "association," in which they condemned the Port Bill in language even more sweeping than that used in their earlier resolutions. In it they also recommended that Virginia and each of the other colonies appoint deputies "to meet in general Congress . . . to deliberate on those . . . measures which the united interests of America may from time to time require." Eighty-nine burgesses, representing nearly three-fourths of the membership of the House, signed the document.

Two days later, after most of the signers of the association had left for home, riders from the north brought fresh news from Massachusetts. On May 13, a Boston town meeting had issued an appeal to the other colonies asking that they not import British goods until Parliament reopened the port of Boston.

The news from Boston called for a quick and positive response, but there were not enough burgesses left in Williamsburg to speak for their absent colleagues. Nor was there any possibility that Dunmore would risk calling the Assembly back into official session. Peyton Randolph, who had served as "moderator" of the Raleigh Tavern group, made the decision "to convene all the Members that were then in Town" and to send for others who lived close enough to assemble quickly.

The next morning, May 30, twenty-five burgesses met at the tavern to discuss the news from Boston. As the record of the meeting shows, the participants agreed that Virginia should "concur with the other Colonies" in a boycott of British goods. Realizing that twenty-five men were too few to speak for the entire colony, they decided to summon all the members of the General Assembly back to Williamsburg in August "to conclude finally on these important Questions,"

This action of the burgesses (like their earlier recommendation for a continental congress), was an extra-legal one and represented a departure from their usual constitutional role. Up to 1774, it had been the king's governor, speaking on behalf of his royal master, who had brought the burgesses together; now a few legislators acting on their own initiative summoned the members of the House for a meeting that would take place without the governor's permission and would conduct its business without him.

The decision of the meeting of May 30 (reproduced in Document #4) was put into writing and signed by Peyton Randolph, George Washington, Thomas Jefferson, and the twenty-two other burgesses present. As a result of their action, meetings were held in the various Virginia counties to choose delegates for the August gathering. In most cases the voters simply reelected the men who had formerly represented them in the House of Burgesses. On August 1, the newly elected burgesses reassembled in Williamsburg as a "convention." The members endorsed the principle of non-importation and elected seven men to represent them in the forthcoming intercolonial congress to be held in Philadelphia a month later.

The August convention was the first of five such gatherings in Virginia. For the next nineteen months—or from August, 1774, to May, 1776,—Virginia was in actuality governed by these conventions. Although the House of Burgesses did reassemble at Dunmore's call in June, 1775, Virginia's official legislature transacted little business of importance. It met at sporadic intervals during the next year and finally adjourned forever on May 6, 1776. Nine days later, Virginia officially declared its independence and so completed the work begun almost two years earlier by a handful of "Representatives" assembled at the Raleigh Tavern.

*   *   *   *

The facsimile of the proceedings is reproduced from the original in the Colonial Papers in the Archives Division, Virginia State Library, Richmond, Virginia.

Resolutions of the Virginia Convention for Independence
May 15, 1776

On May 6, 1776, Virginia's fifth revolutionary convention assembled in Williamsburg with 128 members present. More than a year had passed since British regulars and Massachusetts militiamen had clashed at Lexington, and every succeeding event had intensified the difficulties between England and her colonies. When the Continental Congress raised an army, George III responded by proclaiming his American subjects to be "out of the protection of the British crown," and by sending additional troops to America to put down the insurgents. Lord Dunmore, the king's governor, abandoned his post at Williamsburg and took up arms against the rebellious colonists. During the early months of 1776, various counties throughout Virginia adopted petitions calling for a complete separation from Great Britain.

By the spring of 1776, it was unmistakably clear that the Virginia convention would declare the colony's independence. All that was in doubt was the manner in which the step would be taken. Should Virginia act alone? Or should she join with her sister colonies in the Continental Congress?

The convention, after disposing of some necessary routine business, began to debate the question of independence on May 14. A few members, still hoping for reconciliation with Britain, opposed any immediate action on the matter. Others, like Edmund Pendleton of Caroline County, were ready to declare independence unilaterally and at once. Still others, like Meriwether Smith of

Essex County, were mostly concerned with the need for continuity and for the creation of political institutions to replace those that had become obsolete with the collapse of British authority. Smith therefore proposed that a committee be appointed to prepare "a Declaration of Rights" and "a Plan of Government."

Some representatives, like the fiery Patrick Henry, wanted separation as much as Pendleton but were reluctant to see Virginia act alone. Henry and his followers were convinced that independence could be won only if the colonies acted jointly. He wanted Virginia's delegates in the Continental Congress "to exert their abilities in procuring an immediate, clear & full Declaration of Independency." (This was the first time that any colony had directly instructed its delegates to *initiate* action; other colonies, however, were ready to *support* independence. A month earlier, a North Carolina convention had directed that colony's delegates to "Concur" in any proposal for separation.)

All of these approaches were strenuously debated by the convention, and it fell to Pendelton to reconcile the different ideas. He produced a document that combined Henry's proposal for joint action with Smith's suggestion for a "Plan of Government." His resolutions were acceptable to all parties, including those who had earlier opposed action, and were unanimously adopted.

Pendleton began with a long preamble listing Virginia's grievances against King George III. She and her sister colonies had made "the most decent representations and petitions to the king and parliament" for "a redress of grievances," but their efforts had led only to "increased insult, oppression, and a vigorous attempt to effect our total destruction." The king had raised "Fleets and armies" and hired foreign troops from Germany "to assist these destructive purposes." Dunmore, the king's governor, had taken up arms against Virginians: he had "withheld all the powers of government from operating for our safety" and was "carrying on a piratical and savage war against us." He was tempting the slaves to revolt "and training and employing them against their masters." Because of these hostile acts, the colonists had to choose between

By 1776 colonial opponents of British policy had turned from argument to armed force.

"an abject submission" to the king or "a total separation from the crown and government of Great Britain."

The preamble was followed by two resolutions, the first of which instructed Virginia's delegates in Philadelphia to propose that the Continental Congress "declare the United Colonies free and independent states." The Virginia delegates were also to support measures "for forming foreign alliances and a confederation of the colonies." They were to be careful, however, to make sure that Virginia retained control of her own local affairs: "the power of forming government for, and the regulation of the internal concerns of each colony [were to] be left to the respective colonial legislatures."

The decision to seek "a total separation" meant that Virginia had to develop a new political system, one that would, in Meriwether Smith's words, "be most proper to maintain Peace & Order in this Colony & secure substantial & equal Liberty to the People." Accordingly the resolutions of May 15 also included Smith's proposal that a committee be appointed to prepare a declaration of rights and "a Plan of Government" for the independent new commonwealth he and his colleagues were about to create.

A copy of the resolutions was sent immediately to Philadelphia, and on June 7 Richard Henry Lee, the ranking member of the Virginia delegation in Congress, offered a motion that "these United Colonies are, and of right ought to be, free and independent States." On July 2 the Continental Congress, after long debate, took the step that Virginia had urged, and declared that the people of America were "absolved from all allegiance to the British crown."

*   *   *   *

The facsimile of the Resolutions for Independence is reproduced from a manuscript in the Papers of the Continental Congress in the National Archives, Washington, D. C., and it is copied with the permission of the National Archives.

The Virginia
Declaration of Rights
June 12, 1776

The Virginia convention, in making its decision for independence on May 15, 1776, had ordered that a committee be appointed to "prepare a Declaration of Rights, and . . . a plan of government." On that day George Mason, who was to be the principal author of both documents, was still somewhere on the road between Gunston Hall, his home on the Potomac, and the capital at Williamsburg. The delegate from Fairfax County, his departure delayed by "a smart fit of the Gout," did not take his seat in the convention until May 18. That same day he was named to the committee—already twenty-eight strong—charged with preparing the "Declaration of Rights."

Mason, for all his retiring nature and his reluctance to play a political role, was unusually well fitted for service on the committee. He was the author of the Fairfax Resolves of 1774, in which he had eloquently asserted the rights of the colonists and stoutly challenged British efforts to suppress those rights. His knowledge of political and constitutional history was recognized by most of his colleagues. Drawing on this background, the fifty-one-year-old planter settled down to produce the most significant and most enduring work of his career.

Several other members of the committee made proposals which became part of the final declaration, but it was Mason's plan that—one contemporary later recalled—"swallowed up all the rest, by fixing the grounds" upon which the final document rested.

Despite numerous changes, the sixteen-part declaration, adopted by the convention on June 12, was essentially the work of the scholar from Gunston Hall.

There were various precedents for the declaration to which Mason set his hand, ranging from the English Bill of Rights of 1689 to the Declaration of Rights adopted by the Continental Congress in 1774. The members of the Virginia convention, familiar with the abuses for which the British government of their day was responsible, felt they must endeavor to prevent their own new government from repeating such abuses.

The first three articles of the declaration dealt with fundamental political principles: the first stated that men were created "equally free & independent" and that they possessed "certain inherent Rights." Among these were "the enjoyment of life and liberty, with the means of acquiring and possessing property, and pursuing and obtaining happiness and safety" (Article 1). Some of the more conservative members thought that this language was too sweeping and that Mason's words might tempt the slaves on their plantations to demand liberty for themselves. Mason himself was opposed to slavery, but for the sake of unity he agreed to an amendment of this section. The declaration in its final form stated that men came into possession of their rights only "when they enter into a State of Society." The Virginians who adopted the declaration argued that a slave could not share the benefits of citizenship because he had not truly entered into society.

The Declaration of Rights went on to state that all governmental power was "derived from the People" (Article 2). Whenever any government failed to provide for their "common benefit, protection, and security," the people had "an indubitable, unalienable and indefeasible Right" to change that government or even to abolish it (Article 3).

The remainder of the document was concerned with more specific matters. All public offices were to be filled by election rather than by inheritance and were not to be passed on from father to son (Article 4). The powers of government should be "separated," that is, divided between the legislative, executive, and judicial branches; and there should be "frequent, certain and regular elections" to insure rotation in office (Article 5). Elections were to be free and open to all men who had a "permanent common Interest with, and Attachment to, the Community." Citizens were not to be taxed or subjected to any law "without their own Consent, or that of their Representatives" (Article 6). "The Power of suspending Laws," which English kings had abused so often, was "not to be exercised" (Article 7).

The next four articles were concerned with the legal rights of the individual, many of which had long been accepted in British practice. Every man accused of a crime had a right to "demand the Cause and Nature of his Accusation," to be confronted with his accusers, to present evidence in his own favor, and, most important, to be tried by an impartial jury (Article 8). Jury trials were also declared to be "preferable to any other" in civil cases (Article 11). Excessive bail was forbidden, as were "cruel & unusual punishments" (Article 9), and all search warrants had to describe the thing or person being searched for (Article 10).

At the suggestion of Thomas Ludwell Lee, the declaration also affirmed the freedom of the press—"one of the greatest Bulwalks of Liberty" (Article 12). Standing armies in time of peace were condemned, and the military forces were to be "under strict Subordination" to the civil authorities (Article 13). The declaration also proclaimed that no government "separate from, or independent of, the Government of Virginia" should ever be established "within the Limits" of the commonwealth (Article 14). "The Blessings of Liberty" could be preserved only "by a firm Adherence to Justice, Moderation, Temperance, Frugality, and Virtue" (Article 15). The last section concerned liberty of conscience, and provided for "the free exercise of religion" (Article 16); it was proposed by young James Madison of Orange County.

The Virginia Declaration of Rights, as the author himself noted later, "was afterwards closely imitated" by the other states. Several of them adopted bills of rights within a year after the passage of the Virginia model; the others provided for the protection of personal liberties by including appropriate guarantees in their state constitutions or by statutes. The declaration also helped to provide inspiration for the first ten amendments (1791) to the federal Constitution, and for the French Declaration of the Rights of Man and the Citizen (1789).

In Virginia itself, the Declaration of Rights has always been cherished. Although it has been amended from time to time to meet the changing needs of the people, it has been retained in each of the five constitutions which the commonwealth has adopted since 1776. The version now in force, for example, includes guarantees against racial or religious discrimination and sets forth the basic principle that the government of the state has the obligation to provide "an effective system of education" for all its people.

*   *   *   *

The original draft of Mason's declaration is in the Mason Papers in the Library of Congress; the document reproduced here is from a manuscript in the Archives Division, Virginia State Library, Richmond, Virginia. Although it bears the heading "Copy of the first D[r]aught by G. M.," this document was in fact drawn up in 1778. In it the author incorporated elements of his own earlier draft and those that emerged from the committee on rights and from the full convention. It was presented to the Commonwealth of Virginia in 1844 by John Mason (1766-1849), the only surviving son of George Mason.

All references to the Virginia Declaration in the preceding note, and all quotations from it, are taken from the sixteen-part version adopted by the convention rather than from the fourteen-part manuscript version reproduced in facsimile. The Papers of George Mason, *ed. Robert A. Rutland (Chapel Hill, 1970), I, 287-89, contains the full text.*

A Constitution
or Form of Government
June 29, 1776

Virginia's decision to seek independence from Great Britain meant that the political machinery under which her people had lived for a century and a half was no longer usable. The authority previously exercised by the king through his governors had ceased, and would have to be assumed by some other agency. It had become necessary to create—as quickly as possible—a new government that would, in the words of Edmund Pendleton, provide "Prosperity to the Community and Security to Individuals."

The members of the Virginia convention fully realized the need for action in this matter. In their resolutions of May 15, 1776, they had appointed a committee to draw up both a plan of government and a declaration of rights. Rebellious Americans elsewhere were also aware of the problem of maintaining peace and order in the midst of political upheaval. On the same day that the Virginia convention acted, the Continental Congress passed a resolution urging every colony "to adopt such governments as shall . . . best conduce to the happiness and safety of their constituents." Thus when the Virginia body took steps to adopt a "plan of government" in late June, it did so in pursuance not only of its own orders but also of the recommendations of Congress.

The task of preparing a constitution was entrusted to the same committee which had drawn up the Declaration of Rights. Once that committee had completed work on the declaration, its members turned their attention to the "plan of government." On May

24, Edmund Pendleton, who was not a member of the rights committee but who was closely following its actions, wrote to Thomas Jefferson that "the Political Cooks are busy in preparing the dish." Summer weather had descended upon the Virginia Tidewater, but most members, Pendleton wrote, were prepared "to sweat it out with fortitude." On June 1 he could report that "we build our Government slowly. I hope it will be founded on a Rock."

George Mason submitted his draft of a constitution in mid-June. In the course of debate, it underwent a few minor changes, but most of his original ideas were retained when the convention gave the document its approval on June 29.

The final version did include a major addition to Mason's version. Other Virginians had tried their hand at drafting a constitution for Virginia during the late spring and early summer of 1776. Among them was Thomas Jefferson, then one of Virginia's delegates to the Continental Congress. His draft, which reached Williamsburg late in June, included a preamble which the convention adopted and incorporated as the preamble of their own work.

In this section, Jefferson denounced George III for perverting his "Kingly Office . . . into a detestable and insupportable Tyranny," and went on to list various "acts of Misrule" that the king and Lord Dunmore, the former royal governor, had committed. The purpose of this section was, of course, to justify the convention's decision to establish an independent government.

The constitution called for the legislative, executive, and judicial branches of the new government to be separate "so that neither exercise the Powers properly belonging to the other." In adopting this provision, the convention prevented the development of a parliamentary system like that of England, under which members of the executive (or ministry) hold seats in the legislature. The legislative department was to consist of two houses: a House of Delegates, in which every Virginia county would have equal representation (as in the House of Burgesses which it replaced), and a Senate of twenty-four members. Both houses were to be elected by the people. The executive branch was to consist of a governor "or Chief Magistrate" and an eight-man "Council of State." There would also be a judicial branch, which was to include a Supreme Court of Appeals, a General Court, and other courts.

Yet the three branches were not so completely independent of each other as the idea of separate powers required. The General Assembly was for all practical purposes the predominant branch. In the Assembly, the House of Delegates held most of the power, including the right of initiating legislation; the Senate could only approve, amend, or reject bills passed by the delegates. It was the Assembly which, by joint ballot of the two houses, elected both the governor and the members of the Council of State and appointed all judges of the superior courts.

The makers of the Virginia constitution, remembering their experience with royal governors like Dunmore, deliberately made the office of chief executive weak. The governor could not veto laws passed by the Assembly or dissolve that body as Dunmore and others had done. Finally, the General Assembly could impeach the chief executive whenever he exceeded his authority.

The convention decided to declare the new constitution in force immediately rather than to submit it to the people for their approval. They did so because they felt the times were too critical and the need for establishing a stable government too urgent to permit any delay. In later years, Jefferson and other Virginians criticized the constitution because it had not been subjected to this democratic test.

Critics also pointed to other defects. They particularly objected to the basis of representation in the lower house, in which each county—regardless of its size or its population—had two delegates. This system made it possible for the numerous eastern counties, most of which had a relatively small white population, to maintain control of the legislature and to direct state policy. There were also objections to the fact that the constitution continued to require property qualifications for voting, which meant that many Virginians were disenfranchised.

Nonetheless the 1776 "plan of government" remained in force for over half a century. In 1830, after decades of agitation, Virginia adopted a new constitution; since then, the commonwealth has had four more constitutions: those adopted in 1851, in 1869, in 1902, and most recently in 1971. Each has made alterations in the structure of the state government. Among the major changes have been the adoption of manhood suffrage and the strengthening of the office of the governor (1851), the establishment of statewide public education (1869), and the assertion of state power over business (1902). The House of Delegates is no longer supreme, and the state now undertakes responsibilities and functions undreamed of in 1776. Yet the basic principle has been maintained: the idea of a representative government responsible to the governed and based on fundamental law. Virginians continue to live under a constitution designed to "maintain peace and order" and to "secure substantial and equal liberty to the people."

*   *   *   *

The facsimile of the 1776 constitution is reproduced from the manuscript copy of that document preserved in the Archives Division, Virginia State Library, Richmond, Virginia. This copy was drafted by the clerk of the convention. The markings and underlinings on it suggest that it was used as the basis for the printed version which appeared on July 5, 1776, as a supplement to Alexander Purdie's Virginia Gazette.

A Bill for Establishing Religious Freedom

Proposed, June 12, 1779

Passed, January 16, 1786

In the opinion of the men who adopted the Virginia Declaration of Rights in 1776, every man was "entitled to the free exercise of religion." The declaration, however, was simply a statement of principle; it did not in itself provide a legal basis for liberty of conscience. Anglicanism was still the official religion in Virginia, and every individual, whether he was a member of that faith or not, was still obliged to pay taxes for its support. In order to fulfill the declaration's promise of "a free exercise of religion," it was necessary for Virginians to go beyond the language of Mason's document.

One of the first efforts to fulfill the promise was made by Thomas Jefferson while he was a member of the Second Continental Congress. In the draft he prepared in 1776 for a Virginia constitution, he included an article designed to guarantee religious freedom to the people of the state. "All persons shall have free and full liberty of religious opinion," he wrote at that time; none were to be "compelled to frequent or maintain any religious institution." His article for religious freedom was not adopted, and Virginia's first constitution contained no mention of the subject.

But Jefferson and those who shared his opinions persisted in their efforts to obtain a complete separation of church and state. The first step was taken late in 1776 by the General Assembly. Its "Act for exempting Dissenters" repealed all colonial laws containing penalties for unorthodox religious opinions, abolished most of the special privileges enjoyed up to that time by the Church of England, and, most important, it exempted dissenters (those who were not members of the established church) from paying taxes for the support of that church.

Many Virginians, including dissenters as well as Anglicans, felt the Assembly had, in effect, moved too far toward complete religious freedom. They felt that every man, regardless of his beliefs, should be required by law to contribute to the support of *some* Christian denomination—preferably that to which he himself belonged—and that the state should collect that contribution by taxation. By the end of 1776 the Assembly began receiving petitions asking it to enact a "general assessment" law for the support of religion. The legislature postponed a vote on the issue, but the fact that the matter had been raised convinced Thomas Jefferson and like-minded persons that the Assembly should enact laws that would guarantee full liberty of conscience.

In 1777 Jefferson, who was then helping to revise the commonwealth's code of laws, drafted his celebrated "bill for establishing religious freedom." On June 12, 1779, ten days after he assumed the office of governor, his supporters presented the measure to the House of Delegates.

The bill began with a long and eloquent preamble which affirmed the power of human reason and declared that it was "sinful and tyrannical" for a state "to compel a man to furnish contributions of money" for the support of any religious body. A man's opinion was his own business; there was no reason for any political authority to intervene, even to shield men from bad ideas. "Truth is great and will prevail if left to herself," Jefferson proclaimed; it was "the proper and sufficient antagonist to error."

Jefferson had established the philosophical argument for complete freedom of opinion in his preamble. The bill itself provided that "no man shall be compelled to frequent or support any religious worship, place, or ministry whatsoever." Instead, all were to be "free to profess, and by argument to maintain, their opinions in matters of religion." The bill ended with a declaration that any future attempt to repeal it "or to narrow its operation" would be "an infringement of natural right."

Although many members of the Assembly supported the bill, conservatives of all faiths opposed it as "a diabolical measure," likely to subvert the basis of public morality. After strenuous debate it was tabled; not until 1785 was it brought up again. In the meantime, proposals for a "general assessment" continued to attract support. In 1784 a bill imposing a tax "for the support of the Christian religion" was offered to the Assembly. Eight years earlier James Madison had introduced the idea of a "free exercise of religion" into the Declaration of Rights. Now he led the advocates of religious freedom to defeat assessment. With victory achieved, he decided that the time had come to bring forward Jefferson's proposal once again.

With Madison acting as floor leader, the House of Delegates debated Jefferson's bill through the fall of 1785. It met "warm opposition" in that chamber: some members particularly objected to the preamble with its sweeping and eloquent defense of the power of reason. Nevertheless, the bill itself easily passed the House, 74 to 20 (many of the 156 members present did not vote), and was sent to the Senate. After further debate, the upper house gave its approval, and the bill became law on January 16, 1786.

Supporters of the measure were elated by their success. Madison reported the victory to Jefferson—then living in Paris as American minister to France—and expressed the hope that Virginia, by her action, had "extinguished forever the ambitious hope of making laws for the human mind." Jefferson replied that the law had been "received with infinite approbation in Europe and propogated with enthusiasm" by the people, if not by their rulers. He himself did much to propogate it by having the text translated into French and Italian and seeing to it that copies were widely circulated on the continent. He was proud, he wrote Madison, that Virginia had "produced the first legislature who had the courage to declare that the reason of man may be trusted with the formation of his own opinions."

The act for establishing religious freedom has remained on the Virginia statute books to the present. Its key section (which begins, "no man shall be compelled . . .") has been part of every constitution adopted since the passage of the bill. The newest constitution, ratified in 1971, has incorporated the act into the Bill of Rights itself. Thus Jefferson's statement that "no man shall be compelled to frequent or support any religious worship" is joined to Madison's earlier assertion of "the free exercise of religion."

*   *   *   *

No manuscript draft of Jefferson's bill is known to exist. The version nearest to Jefferson's own was that printed in the Report of the Committee of Revisors, *published at Richmond in 1784, more than a year before the final passage of the bill. The facsimile in this set is taken from pages 58-59 of a copy of the* Report *in the Rare Book Collection, Virginia State Library, Richmond, Virginia; it has been reproduced by combining the relevant portions of the two pages on which the text of the bill appears.*

Resolutions for the Cession of Lands to the United States

January 2, 1781

Document No. 9

At the time that Virginia declared her independence from Great Britain, the colony extended westward beyond the Allegheny Mountains to the Mississippi River. Within these bounds lay a vast expanese of territory, largely uninhabited by white men, that comprised over a quarter million square miles and stretched north from the Ohio River to the Great Lakes.

Virginia's claim to this region was based on the charter issued to the London Company in 1609 by King James I, and the state had specifically asserted her claim to the territory in the constitution adopted in 1776. Two years later, in the summer of 1778, her citizens had actually taken physical possession of the region when a military force under Colonel George Rogers Clark seized the principal British posts north of the Ohio.

Virginia's claims to the lands north of the Ohio River were not unchallenged. Several other states (particularly Connecticut and Massachusetts) claimed parts of the region, while those states like Maryland that had no western territories of their own protested the claims of the states that did. Maryland knew that states owning large areas of uninhabited lands could raise a large part of their revenue by selling land to prospective settlers, while states without such holdings would have to tax their citizens more heavily in order to raise revenue. The landholdings of the larger states seemed to threaten the economic development of the smaller states; the latter feared their citizens would move into states having fewer and lower taxes. For this and other reasons, the Maryland legislature refused to ratify the Articles of Confederation until Virginia and other landholding states ceded their western territory to the central government for the benefit of all American citizens. Since the Articles (which Virginia had ratified in December, 1777) could not go into effect until every state had accepted them, the struggling new nation remained without a formal government. By the closing years of the Revolution, the opposition of the "have-not" states was threatening the common cause of continental unity.

On September 6, 1780, the Continental Congress passed a resolution calling on Virginia and the other states with western lands to make "a liberal surrender" of their claims, so as "to establish the federal union on a fixed and permanent basis." Two of Virginia's delegates in Congress took immediate action to protect their state's interest in the western country and to provide for the region's political development. Joseph Jones presented a motion, which James Madison had helped to prepare, spelling out the terms under which Virginia was willing to give up the Illinois territory: Congress was to guarantee Virginia's claims to the lands south of the Ohio River, and was to agree to lay out the territory north of the river into "separate and distinct states," having equal rights with the existing thirteen. On October 10 Congress accepted these and other conditions imposed by Virginia.

Governor Jefferson officially informed the General Assembly of Congress's action early in November, but the members did not take up the matter until January 1, 1781. On the same day, news came that a British fleet was on its way up the James River to attack Richmond. The Assembly took time in the emergency to adopt resolutions concerning the Northwest Territory and then adjourned; the members dispersed to their homes just three days before the invading British moved into Richmond.

The Assembly's resolutions began with a statement that "the happiness, strength and safety" of the United States depended upon the ratification of the Articles of Confederation: the good of the country was "preferable to every object of smaller importance."

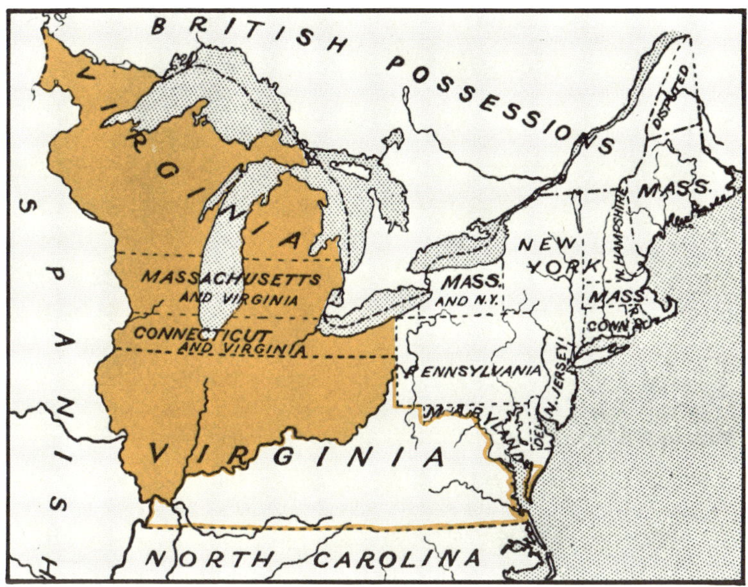

The area shown in outline on this map indicates the territory claimed by Virginia until its cession of the Northwest Territory; the shaded portion shows the territory that was given up to the United States.

Virginia was ready, for the benefit of the United States, to yield all her rights in the lands north of the Ohio River.

The resolutions included a number of conditions, most of which had appeared in the Jones-Madison motion to Congress. Virginia was to be reimbursed for the expenses she had incurred in conquering the area from the British in 1778 and "in maintaining Garrisons and supporting civil Government" there. The civil rights of the inhabitants of Kaskaskia and Vincennes, most of them of French ancestry, were to be guaranteed. Clark and his men were to receive land grants in the area, as the Virginia General Assembly had previously promised them.

In making the cession the Virginia legislature included an even more important stipulation. The ceded territory was to be "formed into . . . distinct republican states . . . having the same rights of sovereignty, freedom and independence as the other states." This reservation was derived from an idea advanced by Jefferson in his draft constitution of 1776 and incorporated in the Jones-Madison motion accepted by Congress in October of 1780.

Virginia's sacrifice of her western lands in the cause of American unity bore almost immediate fruit. Within a month the Maryland Assembly gave its blessing to the Articles of Confederation, and on March 1 the Maryland delegates in Congress formally signed the document, bringing it finally into operation.

Three more years passed before Congress settled on the detailed terms of the Virginia cession. The formal deed was completed and accepted by Congress early in 1784. It provided that all unallotted lands in the region be held "as a common fund" for the benefit of the whole country, and it promised eventual statehood to the people of the new territory. The Confederation Congress made its final arrangements for the administration of the Northwest Territory by its passage of the Northwest Ordinance in 1787. Between 1803 and 1848 five new states—Ohio, Indiana, Illinois, Michigan, and Wisconsin—were formed from the area between the Ohio and the Great Lakes.

Largely because of her cession, Virginia has long been known as the "mother of states." Of more significance, however, is the manner in which Virginia made the cession and set the pattern for the development of the American nation. Whereas England had kept her colonies subordinate to the home island and denied them a chance to gain political equality with the mother country, the United States has permitted her territories to join the union on an equal basis with the original thirteen states.

*   *   *   *

The original draft of the resolutions, from which this facsimile is reproduced, is filed with the Rough Bills of the House of Delegates for the session of 1780/81, in the Archives Division, Virginia State Library, Richmond, Virginia.

Form of Ratification
of the Constitution
June 25, 1788

DOCUMENT NO. 10

The union created by the Articles of Confederation in 1781 was more like a loose alliance of independent states than a nation. The defects in the new government became obvious so quickly that men soon began discussing means of revising and reforming the Articles. The central government had no real executive or judicial powers, and the powers of the legislature—the Congress of the Confederation—were few. Congress lacked the means of forcing either the states or the citizens to carry out its decisions. For its revenues it had to depend upon contributions or "quotas" from the states: it lacked authority to tax citizens directly. It had no control over either interstate or foreign commerce: each state set its own commercial policy, often without regard to the welfare of neighboring states or the overall interests of the nation.

As dissension developed between the various states, some Americans began to fear a complete collapse of the Confederation. In the fall of 1786, George Washington, writing to James Madison, lamented that the country was "fast verging to anarchy and confusion"; the states, he observed, were "pulling against each other, and all tugging at the federal head."

Virginians like Washington and Madison were among the first to recognize the weaknesses of the Articles and to seek for ways to strengthen them. Partly as a result of their leadership, the other states agreed to appoint delegates to a convention to be held in Philadelphia in May of 1787.

Although the Philadelphia convention was empowered only to revise the Articles, there emerged from it a completely new plan of government. The proposed Constitution of the United States provided for a central government that would be much more powerful than that of the Confederation. It was to consist of three separate branches: a two-house legislature to make laws, an executive department to carry out and enforce the laws, and a judicial wing to settle disputes arising under the laws. The new government would have the power to tax American citizens directly and to control both interstate and foreign commerce.

The Constitution was not to go into effect until it had been ratified by nine states. By June, 1788, eight of them had given it their approval and on June 21, New Hampshire also ratified. The success of the new form of government nevertheless depended upon two states with large populations—Virginia and New York—neither of which had yet reached a decision. The approval of Virginia was particularly crucial: most Americans realized that a union without the Old Dominion would be no real union.

In both states public opinion was so divided that ratification was considerably in doubt. On October 25, 1787, the Virginia General Assembly had directed that the proposed constitution be submitted to a special state convention. Elections for delegates to the convention were held throughout the state in March of the following year. In the course of the campaign, Virginia voters heard arguments for and against ratification. The results of the election were so close that few observers ventured to predict the outcome of the convention's deliberations.

On June 3, one hundred and seventy delegates, two from each of the eighty-four counties of the state and one from each of the boroughs of Norfolk and Williamsburg, met in Richmond. For three weeks they discussed the Constitution, article by article, section by section. Leading the fight for acceptance was James Madison; the principal opponents were George Mason and Patrick Henry.

Most of the arguments voiced for or against ratification in the

Virginia convention had been made earlier in newspapers and pamphlets and in other state conventions. The men who opposed acceptance feared that the central government would become so powerful that the states would lose control of their own affairs. Many also objected to the new Constitution because it did not include a bill of rights.

On June 25 the debate came to an end and the delegates proceeded to the final vote. Before the convention were two sets of resolutions. One proposed that Virginia withhold her approval of the Constitution until it was amended; the other called for immediate ratification without condition. Those who opposed a delay feared that the attempt to achieve prior amendment might "bring the Union into danger." Yet they realized they should make some concession "to relieve the apprehensions" of those who feared the potential power of the central government. In proposing that the convention ratify the Constitution, they also recommended that the Congress "which shall first assemble under the said Constitution" make amendments to safeguard the rights of the people and of the states. Their resolutions passed, by a narrow majority of ten votes, on the morning of June 25.

Two committees were immediately appointed: one to draw up a "form of ratification"; the other "to prepare and report" a set of amendments. Among those named to the committee to prepare the "form of ratification" were Governor Edmund Randolph, James Madison, and John Marshall (later chief justice of the United States). On that same day they submitted their report. It began with a declaration that "the powers granted under the Constitution" were "derived from the people of the United States" and were to be resumed by them if the new federal government ever sought to use its authority to injure or oppress them. The federal government was not to abridge or restrain any right except in such instances as were specifically provided for by the Constitution, and it was not to restrict such "essential rights" as "Liberty of Conscience and of the Press" under any condition whatsoever. The document concluded with an unequivocal declaration "in the name and behalf of the People of Virginia" that "the said Constitution is binding upon the said people."

In this way Virginia became the tenth state to accept the Constitution. Her decision undoubtedly aided the cause of ratification in New York, which approved the new union in July. When the first Congress of the United States assembled in New York City the following spring, eleven of the thirteen states were represented. A year later the two remaining states, North Carolina and Rhode Island, had also decided to join the Union.

Meanwhile the movement to add a bill of rights was underway. By September, 1789, the first Congress had begun to discuss possible amendments. Acting under the leadership of James Madison and drawing on proposals made by Virginia and other states, it prepared twelve amendments and submitted them to the state legislatures for approval. During the next two years, ten of the twelve were ratified by the states; in 1791 they became the first ten amendments to the Constitution.

Virginia, by ratifying the Constitution, had helped to make possible a stronger and more effective national government; by insisting on amendments, the commonwealth helped to make that government more mindful of the rights of the governed.

*   *   *   *

The form of ratification reproduced here is copied from the first two pages of a bound manuscript in the Archives Division, Virginia State Library, Richmond, Virginia. The remainder of the manuscript comprises the text of the Constitution itself.

Appendix

and

Bibliographical Essay

The Texts of the Documents

Document No. 1
AN ORDINANCE AND CONSTITUTION FOR A
COUNCIL AND ASSEMBLY IN VIRGINIA

JULY 24, 1621

To all people to whom these presents shall come, bee seen or heard, the Treasuror, Council and Company of Adventurers and Planters of the Citty of London for the First Collony in Virginia send greeting: knowe yee that wee, the said Treasuror, Counsell and Company, takeing into our carefull consideracion the present state of the said Colony in Virginia, and intending by the Devine assistance to settle such a forme of government ther as may bee to the greatest benifltt and comfort of the people and wherby all injustice, grevance and oppression may bee prevented and kept of as much as is possible from the said Colony, have thought fitt to make our entrance by ordaining & establishing such supreame Counsells as may not only bee assisting to the Governor for the time being in administracion of justice and the executing of other duties to his office belonging, but also by ther vigilent care & prudence may provide as well for remedy of all inconveniencies groweing from time to time as also for the advancing of encrease, strengthe, stabillitie and prosperitie of the said Colony:

Wee therefore, the said Treasuror, Counsell and Company, by authoritie directed to us from His Majestie under his Great Seale, upon mature deliberacion doe hereby order & declare that from hence forward ther bee towe supreame Counsells in Virginia for the better government of the said Colony as aforesaid: the one of which Counsells to bee called the Counsell of State and whose office shall cheiflie bee assisting, wth ther care, advise & circomspection, to the said Governor; shall be chosen, nominated, placed and displaced from time to time by us, the said Treasurer, Counsell & Company and our successors; which Counsell of State shall consiste for the present onlie of those persons whose names are here inserted, vizt: Sir Francis Wyatt, Governor of Virginia; Captaine Francis West; Sir George Yeardley, Knight; Sir William Newce, Knight, Marshall of Virginia;

55

Mr. George Sandys, Tresuror; Mr. George Thorpe, Deputy of the Colledge; Captaine Thomas Newce, Deputy for the Company; Mr. Christopher Davison, Secretarie; Doctor Potts, Phesition to the Company; Mr. Paulet; Mr. Leech; Captaine Nathaniell Powell; Mr. Roger Smith; Mr. John Berkley; Mr. John Rolfe; Mr. Ralfe Hamer; Mr. John Pountus; Mr. Michael Lapworth; Mr. Harwood; [and] Mr. Samuel Macocke. Which said Counsellors and Counsell wee earnestlie pray & desier, and in His Majesties name strictlie charge and command, that all factious parcialties and sinister respects laid aside, they bend ther care and endeavors to assist the said Governor first and principallie in advancement of the honor and service of Almightie God and the enlargement of His kingdome amongste those heathen people; and next in the erecting of the said Colonie in one obedience to His Majestie and all lawful authoritie from His Majestis dirived; and lastlie in maitaining the said people in justice and Christian conversation among themselves and in strength and habillitie to wth stand ther ennimies. And this Counsell is to bee alwaies, or for the most part, residing about or neere the said Governor. The other Counsell, more generall, to bee called by the Governor, and yeerly, of course, & no oftner but for very extreordinarie & important occasions, shall consist for present of the said Counsell of State and of tow burgesses out of every towne, hunder [hundred] and other particuler plantacion to bee respetially chosen by the inhabitants. Which Counsell shalbee called the Generall Assemblie, wherein as also in the said Counsell of State, all matters shall be decided, determined & ordered by the greater part of the voices then present, reserveing alwaies to the Governor a negative voice. And this Generall Assembly shall have free power to treat, consult & conclude as well of all emergent occasions concerning the pupliqe weale of the said Colony and evrie parte therof as also to make, ordeine & enact such generall lawes & orders for the behoof of the said Colony and the good govermt therof as shall time to time appeare necessarie or requisite. Wherin as in all other things wee requier the said Gennerall Assembly, as also the said Counsell of State, to imitate and followe the policy of the forme of goverment, lawes, custome, manners of loyall and other administracion of justice used in the realme of England, as neere as may bee even as ourselves by His Majesties lettres patents are required; provided that noe lawes or ordinance made in the said Generall Assembly shalbe and continew in force and validitie, unlese the same shalbe sollemlie ratified and confirmed in a generall greater court of the said court here in England and so ratified and returned to them under our seale. It being our intent to affoord the like measure also unto the said Colony that after the goverment of the [said Colony, shall once have been well framed & settled accordingly, which is to be done by us as by authoritie derived from] his Majestie and the sa[me shall] have bene soe by us declared, no orders of our court afterwarde shall binde [the said] Colony unles they bee ratified in like manner in ther Generall Assembly.

In wittnes wherof wee have hereunto sett our common seale the 24th day of [July] 1621, and in the yeare of the raigne of our governoure, Lord James by the . . . of God of England, Scotland, France & Ireland, King, Defendor of the . . . vizt., of England, France and Scotland the nineteenth and of Scotland the fower and fiftieth.

DOCUMENT No. 2
THE DECLARATION OF THE PEOPLE
AGAINST SIR WILLIAM BERKELEY

JULY 30, 1676

For having upon specious Pretences of publick Works raised unjust Taxes upon the Commonaltie, For advancing of Private Favourites. And other sinister Ends, but noe visible Effect, in any measure adequate.

For not having during the Long time of his Government, In any Measure advanced this hopefull Colonie, either by Fortifications, Towns, or Trade.

For having abused and rendered Contemptable his Maties. Justice, by advancing to Places of Judicature Scandalous and ignorant Favourites.

For having wronged his Maties. Prorogative, and Interest by assuming the Monopolie of the Bever Trade.

For having in that unjust Gaine, betrayed and sold His Maties. Countrie, and the Liberties of his Loyall Subjects to the Barbarous Heathen.

For having Protected, favoured, and Emboldened the Indians against his Maties. most Loyall Subjects; never Contriving, requiring or appointing any due or proper Meanes of Satisfaction for theire many Incursions, Murthers, and Robberies Committed upon Us.

For having when the Armie of the English was upon the Track of the Indians, which now in all Places, burne, spoile, and Murder, And

when Wee might with ease have destroyed them, who were in open
hostilitie.

For having expresslie countermanded, and sent back our Armie by
Passing his word for the Peaceable demeanours of the said Indians,
who Immediately prosecuted their Evill Intentions, Committing horrid
Murders and Robberies, in all Places, being Protected by the said
Engagement and Word passed by Him the said Sr. Wm. Berkeley,
having Ruined and made Desolate a greate Part of his Maties. Countrie, having now drawne Themselfes into such obscure and remote
places, and are by theire Success soe Emboldened and Confirmed, and
by theire Confederates Strengthened. That the Cryes of Blood are in
all Places, and the Terror and Consternation of the People soe greate,
That They are not only become difficult, but a very formidable Enemie
Who might with Ease have been destroyed.

When upon the loud outcries of Blood the Assemblie had with all
Care raised and framed an Armie for the Prevention of future Mis-
cheifs, and Safeguard of his Maties. Colonie.

For having only with the Privacie of a fewe favourites without the
acquainting of the People, only by Alteration of a Figure forged a
Commission, by I Know not what hand, not only without, but against
the Consent of the People, for the Raising and Effecting of Civill
Warr, and Destruction, which being happilie and without Bloodshed
prevented.

For having the second time attempted the Same, thereby calling
down our forces from the Defence of the frontiers, and most weakened
and Exposed Places, for the prevention of Civill Mischiefe and Ruine
amongst our selves; whilst the Barborous Enemie in all places did
Invade Murder and Spoile Us, his Maties. Loyall Subjects.

Of these the aforesaid Articles, Wee accuse Sr. Wm. Berkeley as
guiltie of Each and Everie of the Same, As one Who hath Traiterouslie
attempted, violated and Injured his Maties. Interest here, by the Loss
of a greate Part of his Maties. Colony and many of his faithfull and
Loyal Subjects, by Him betrayed in a Barbarous and shamefull
Manner exposed to the Incursion and Murder of the Heathen.

And We farther declare the Ensueing Persons in this List to have
bin his wicked and Pernicious Councellors and Confederates, Aiders
and Assistants against the Commonaltie in these our Civill Commo-
tions

Sr. Henrie Chicehly	Nich. Spencer
Col. Christopr. Wormly	Joseph Bridger
Phillip Ludwell	Wm. Claybourne

Robert Beverlie
Richard Lee
Thomas Ballard
Wm. Sherwood
Wm. Cole
Richd. Whitecar.

Thom. Hawkins
Math. Kemp
Jon. Page, Clerk
Jon. Cliffe, Clerk
Hub. Farrill
John West

Tho. Reade

And we farther Command that the said Sr. Wm. Berkeley, with all the Persons in this List bee forthwith delivered upp, or Surrender Themselves, within foure dayes after the notice hereof, or otherwise Wee declare as followeth,

That in whatsoever place, House, or Shipp, any of the said Persons shall Reside, bee hid, or protected, Wee doe declare the Owners, Masters and Inhabitants of the said Parties, to bee Confederate Traytors to the People of the Estates of them, and alsoe of all the aforesaid Persons, to be Conficscated, this Wee the Commons of Virginia doe declare.

Desiring a firme union among our Selves, that Wee may Joyntly and with one accord defend our Selves against the Common Enemie, and lett not the faults of the Guiltie be the Reproach of the Innocent, or the faults and Crimes of the Oppressors devide and Sepperate Us Who have Suffered by theire oppressions.

These are therefore in his Maties. Name to Command you forthwith to Seize the Persons above mentioned, as Traytors to the King, and Countrie, and Them to bring to the Middle Plantations, and there to Secure them till further Order and in Case of opposition, if you want any farther Assistance, you are forthwith to demand It In the Name of the People in all the Counties of Virginia.

Nathaniell Bacon
Generall by the Consent of the People.

DOCUMENT No. 3
PATRICK HENRY'S RESOLUTIONS AGAINST THE STAMP ACT

MAY 30, 1765

Resolved That the first Adventurers and Settlers of this his Majesties Colony and Dominion brought with them and transmitted to their Posterity and all other his Majesties Subjects since inhabiting in this his Majestie's said Colony all the Priviledges, Franchises and

Immunities that have at any Time been held, enjoyed, and possessed by the People of Great Britain.

Resolved That by two royal Charters granted by King James the first the Colonists aforesaid are declared intitled to all the Priviledges, Liberties and Immunities of Denizens and natural born Subjects to all Intents and Purposes as if they had been abiding and born within the Realm of England.

Resolved That the Taxation of the People by themselves or by Persons chosen by themselves to represent them, who can only know what Taxes the People are able to bear and the easiest Mode of raising them and are equally affected by such Taxes Themselves is the distinguishing Characteristick of British Freedom and without which the ancient Constitution cannot subsist.

Resolved That his Majestie's liege People of this most ancient Colony have uninteruptedly enjoyed the Right of being thus governed by their own Assembly in the Article of their Taxes and internal Police and that the same hath never been forfeited or any other Way given up but hath been constantly recognized by the Kings and People of Great Britain.

Resolved Therefore that the General Assembly of this Colony have the *only and sole exclusive* Right and Power to lay Taxes and Impositions upon the Inhabitants of this Colony and that every Attempt to vest such Power in any Person or Persons whatsoever other than the General Assembly aforesaid has a manifest Tendency to destroy British as well as American Freedom.

[The transcript of these resolutions is endorsed on the back by Henry as follows:]

The within Resolutions passed the House of Burgesses in May 1765. They formed the first Opposition to the Samp Act and the Scheme of taxing America by the British Parliament. All the Colonys, either thro Fear, or want of Opportunity to form an Opposition, or from Influence of some Kind or other, had remained silent. I had been for the first Time elected a Burgess a few Days before, was young, inexperienced, unacquainted with the Forms of the House and the Members that composed it. Finding the men of Weight averse to Opposition, and the Commencement of the Tax at Hand, and that no person was likely to step forth, I determined to venture, and alone, unadvised, and unassisted, on a blank Leaf of an old Law Book wrote the within. Upon offering them to the House violent Debates ensued. Many Threats were uttered, and much Abuse cast on me by the party for Submission. After a long and warm Contest the Resolutions passed by a very small Majority, perhaps of one or two only. The Alarm spread throughout America with astonishing Quickness, and the ministerial party were overwhelmed. The great point of Resistance to british Taxation was universally established in the Colonys. This brought on the War which finally separated the two Countrys and gave Independence to ours. Whether this will prove a Blessing or a Curse, will depend upon the Use our people make of the Blessings which a gracious God hath bestowed on us. If they are wise, they will be great and happy. If they are of a contrary Character, they will be miserable. Righteousness alone can exalt them as a Nation .

Reader! whoever thou art, remember this, and in thy Sphere, practice Virtue thyself, and encourage it in others.

P. Henry

DOCUMENT No. 4
PROCEEDINGS OF A MEETING OF REPRESENTATIVES
MAY 30, 1774

30th May 1774

At a Meeting of 25 of the late Representatives legally assembled by the Moderator, it was agreed

That Letters be wrote to all our Sister Colonies, acknowledging the Receipt of the Letters and Resolves from Boston &c. informing them, that before the same came to hand, the Virginia Assembly had been unexpectedly dissolved, and most of the Members returned to their respective Counties.

That it is the Opinion of all the late House of Burgesses who could be convened on the present Occasion, that the Colony of Virginia will concur with the other Colonies in such Measures as shall be judged most effectual for the Preservation of the Common Rights and Liberty of British America; that they are of Opinion particularly that an Association against Importations will probably be entered into, as soon as the late Representatives can be collected, and perhaps against Exportations also after a certain Time. But that this must not be considered as an Engagement on the part of this Colony, which it would be presumption in us to enter into, and that we are sending Dispatches to call together the late Representatives to meet at Williamsburg on the first Day of August next to conclude finally on these important Questions.

Peyton Randolph, Moderator.	Mann Page Junr.	Wm Langhorne
Ro. C. Nicholas	Chars. Carter Senr:	T Blackburn
Edmd Pendleton	Js. Mercer	Edmd Berkeley
Will: Harwood	R Wormeley Carter	Jno. Donelson
Richd Adams	G: Washington	P. Carrington
Thom Whiting	Francis Lightfoot Lee	Lewis Burwell
Henry Lee	Thos Nelson jr.	(Gloster)
Lemuel Riddick	R Rutherford	
Th: Jefferson	John Walker	
	James Wood.	

DOCUMENT No. 5

RESOLUTIONS OF THE VIRGINIA CONVENTION FOR INDEPENDENCE

MAY 15, 1776

In Convention May the 15th 1776.
Present one hundred and twelve Members.

Forasmuch as all the endeavours of the United Colonies by the most decent representations and petitions to the king and parliament of Great Britain to restore peace and security to America under the British government and a re-union with that people upon just and liberal terms instead of a redress of grievances have produced from an imperious and vindictive administration increased insult oppression and a vigorous attempt to effect our total destruction. By a late act, all these colonies are declared to be in rebellion, and out of the protection of the British crown our properties subjected to confiscation, our people, when captivated, compelled to join in the murder and plunder of their relations and countrymen, and all former rapine and oppression of Americans declared legal and just. Fleets and armies are raised, and the aid of foreign troops engaged to assist these destructive purposes: The king's representative in this colony hath not only withheld all the powers of government from operating for our safety, but, having retired on board an armed ship, is carrying on a piratical and savage war against us tempting our slaves by every artifice to resort to him, and training and employing them against their masters. In this state of extreme danger, we have no alternative left but an abject submission to the will of those over-bearing tyrants, or a total separation from the crown and government of Great Britain, uniting and exerting the strength of all America for defence, and forming alliances with foreign powers for commerce and aid in war: Wherefore, appealing to the Searcher of Hearts for the sincerity of former declarations, expressing our desire to preserve the connection with that nation, and that we are driven from that inclination by their wicked councils, and the eternal laws of self-preservation.

Resolved unanimously, that the delegates appointed to represent this colony in General Congress be instructed to propose to that respectable body to declare the United Colonies free and independent states, absolved from all allegiance to, or dependence upon, the crown or parliament of Great Britain; and that they give the assent of this colony to such declaration, and to whatever measures may be thought proper and necessary by the Congress for forming foreign alliances and a confederation of the colonies, at such time, and in the manner, as to them shall seem best: Provided, that the power of forming government for, and the regulations of the internal concerns of each colony, be left to the respective colonial legislatures.

Resolved unanimously, that a committee be appointed to prepare a Declaration of Rights, and such a plan of government as will be most likely to maintain peace and order in this colony, and secure substantial and equal liberty to the people.

a Copy   EDMD. PENDLETON P.

JOHN TAZEWELL
Clerk of the Convention

DOCUMENT No. 6
THE VIRGINIA DECLARATION OF RIGHTS

JUNE 12, 1776

(Copy of the first Draught by G. M.)

A Declaration of Rights made by the Representatives of the good People of Virginia, assembled in full and free Convention; which Rights do pertain to them and their Posterity, as the Basis and Foundation of Government.

1. That all Men are created equally free and independent, and have certain inherent natural Rights, of which they cannot, by any Compact, deprive or divest their Posterity; among which are the Enjoyment of Life and Liberty, with the Means of acquiring and possessing Property, and pursuing and obtaining Happiness and Safety.

2. That all Power is by God and Nature vested in, and consequently derived from the People; that Magistrates are their Trustees and Servants, and at all Times amenable to them.

3. That Government is, or ought to be, instituted for the common Benefit, Protection, and Security of the People, Nation, or Community. Of all the various Modes and Forms of Government that is best, which is capable of producing the greatest Degree of Happiness and Safety, and is most effectually secured against the Danger of Mal-Administration; and that whenever any Government shall be found inadequate or contrary to these Purposes, a Majority of the Community hath an indubitable, unalienable, and indefeasible Right to reform, alter, or abolish it, in such Manner as shall be judged most conducive to the Public Weal.

4. That no Man, or Set of Men, are entitled to exclusive or separate Emoluments or Privileges from the Community, but in Consideration of public Services; which not being descendible, neither ought the Offices of Magistrate, Legislator, or Judge, to be hereditary.

5. That the legislative and executive Powers of the State should be separate and distinct from the judicial; and that the members of the two first may be restrained from Oppression, by feeling and participating the Burthens of the People, they should, at fixed Periods, be reduced to a private Station, and return into that Body from which they were originally taken; and the Vacancys be supplied by frequent, certain and regular Elections.

6. That Elections of Members, to serve as Representatives of the People in the Legislature, ought to be free, and that all Men having sufficient Evidence of permanent common Interest with, and Attachment to the Community, have the Right of Suffrage; and can not be taxed, or deprived of their Property for public Uses, without their own Consent, or that of their Representatives so elected, nor bound by any Law to which they have not, in like Manner, assented for the common Good.

7. That all Power of Suspending Laws, or the Execution of Laws, by any Authority, without Consent of the Representatives of the People, is injurious to their Rights, and ought not to be exercised.

8. That in all capital or criminal Prosecutions, a Man hath a Right to demand the Cause and Nature of his Accusation to be confronted with the Accusers and Witnesses, to call for Evidence in his Favour, and to a speedy Trial by an impartial Jury of his Vicinage, without whose unanimous Consent He can not be found guilty, nor can he be compelled to give Evidence against himself; and that no Man be

deprived of his Liberty, except by the Law of the Land, or the Judgment of his Peers.

9. That excessive Bail ought not to be required, nor excessive Fines imposed, nor cruel and unusual Punishments inflicted.

10. That in Controversies respecting Property, and in Suits between Man and Man, the ancient Trial by Jury is preferable to any other, and ought to be held sacred.

11. That the Freedom of the Press is one of the great Bulwarks of Liberty, and can never be restrained but by despotic Governments.

12. That a well regulated Militia, composed of the Body of the People trained to Arms, is the proper, natural, and safe Defence of a free State; that Standing Armies, in Time of Peace, should be avoided, as dangerous to Liberty; and that, in all cases, the military should be under strict Subordination to, and governed by the civil Power.

13. That no free Government, or the Blessing of Liberty, can be preserved to any People, but by a firm Adherence to Justice, Moderation, Temperance, Frugality and Virtue, and by frequent Recurrence to fundamental Principles.

14. That Religion, or the Duty which we owe to our Creator, and the Manner of discharging it, can be directed only by Reason and Conviction, not by Force or Violence, and therefore that all Men should enjoy the fullest Toleration in the Exercise of Religion, according to the Dictates of Conscience, unpunished, and unrestrained by the Magistrate; unless under Colour of Religion, any Man disturb the Peace, the Happiness, or the Safety of Society. And that it is the mutual Duty of all to practise Christian Forbearance, Love, and Charity towards each other.

[Mason added the following note to the text of this "Copy":]

This Declaration of Rights was the first in America; it received few Alterations or Additions in the Virginia Convention (some of them not for the better) and was afterwards closely imitated by the other United States.

DOCUMENT NO. 7

A CONSTITUTION, OR FORM OF GOVERNMENT

JUNE 29, 1776

In a General Convention.

Begun and holden at the Capitol, in the City of Williamsburg, on Monday the sixth day of May, one thousand seven hundred and seventy six, and continued, by adjournments to the   day of June following:

A Constitution, or form of Government,

agreed to and resolved upon by the Delegates and Representatives of the several Counties and Corporations of Virginia.

Whereas George the Third, King of Great Britain and Ireland, and Elector of Hanover, heretofore intrusted with the exercise of the Kingly Office in this Government, hath endeavoured to pervert the same into a detestable and insupportable Tyranny; by putting his negative on laws the most wholesome and necessary for the publick good;

by denying his Governours permission to pass Laws of immediate and pressing importance, unless suspended in their operation for his assent, and, when so suspended, neglecting to attend to them for many Years;

by refusing to pass certain other laws, unless the persons to be benefited by them would relinquish the inestimable right of representation in the legislature;

by dissolving legislative assemblies repeatedly and continually, for opposing with manly firmness his invasions of the rights of the people;

when dissolved, by refusing to call others for a long space of time, thereby leaving the political system without any legislative head;

by endeavouring to prevent the population of our Country, and, for that purpose, obstructing the laws for the naturalization of foreigners;

by keeping among us, in times of peace, standing Armies and Ships of War;

by affecting to render the Military independent of, and superiour to, the civil power;

by combining with others to subject us to a foreign Jurisdiction, giving his assent to their pretended Acts of Legislation;

for quartering large bodies of armed troops among us;

for cutting off our Trade with all parts of the World;

for imposing Taxes on us without our Consent;

for depriving us of the Benefits of Trial by Jury;

for transporting us beyond Seas, to be tried for pretended Offences;

for suspending our own Legislatures, and declaring themselves invested with power to legislate for us in all Cases whatsoever;

by plundering our Seas, ravaging our Coasts, burning our Towns, and destroying the lives of our People;

by inciting insurrections of our fellow Subjects, with the allurements of forfeiture and confiscation;

by prompting our Negroes to rise in Arms among us, those very negroes whom, by an inhuman use of his negative, he hath refused us permission to exclude by Law;

by endeavouring to bring on the inhabitants of our Frontiers the merciless Indian savages, whose known rule of Warfare is an undistinguished Destruction of all Ages, Sexes, and Conditions of Existance;

by transporting, at this time, a large Army of foreign Mercenaries, to compleat the Works of Death, desolation, and Tyranny, already begun with circumstances of Cruelty and Perfidy unworthy the head of a civilized Nation;

by answering our repeated Petitions for Redress with a Repetition of Injuries;

and finally, by abandoning the Helm of Government, and declaring us out of his Allegiance and Protection;

By which several Acts of Misrule, the Government of this Country, as formerly exercised under the Crown of Great Britain, is totally dissolved; We therefore, the Delegates and Representatives of the good People of Virginia, having maturely considered the Premises, and viewing with great concern the deplorable condition to which this once happy Country must be reduced, unless some regular adequate Mode of civil Polity is speedily adopted, and in Compliance with a Recommendation of the General Congress, do ordain and declare the future Form of Government of Virginia to be as followeth:

The legislative, executive, and judiciary departments, shall be separate and distinct, so that neither exercise the Powers properly belonging to the other; nor shall any person exercise the powers of more than one of them at the same time, except that the Justices of the County Courts shall be eligible to either House of Assembly.

The legislative shall be formed of two distinct branches, who, together, shall be a complete Legislature. They shall meet once, or oftener, every Year, and shall be called the General Assembly of Virginia.

One of these shall be called the House of Delegates, and consist of two Representatives to be chosen for each County, and for the District of West Augusta, annually, of such Men as actually reside in and are freeholders of the same, or duly qualified according to Law, and also of one Delegate or Representative to be chosen annually for the City of Williamsburg, and one for the Borough of Norfolk, and a Representative for each of such other Cities and Boroughs, as may here-after be allowed particular Representation by the legislature; but when any City or Borough shall so decrease as that the number of persons having right of Suffrage therein shall have been for the space of seven Years successively less than half the number of Voters in some one County in Virginia, such City or Borough thenceforward shall cease to send a Delegate or Representative to the Assembly.

The other shall be called the Senate, and consist of twenty four Members, of whom thirteen shall constitute a House to proceed on Business for whose election the different Counties shall be divided into twenty four districts, and each County of the respective District, at the time of the election of its Delegates, shall vote for one Senator, who is actually a resident and freeholder within the District, or duly qualified according to Law, and is upwards of twenty five Years of Age; And the sheriff of each County, within five days at farthest after the last County election in the District, shall meet at some convenient place, and from the Poll so taken in their respective Counties return as a Senator to the House of Senators the Man who shall have the greatest number of Votes in the whole District. To keep up this Assembly by rotation, the Districts shall be equally divided into four Classes, and numbered by Lot. At the end of one Year after the General Election, the six Members elected by the first division shall be displaced, and the vacancies thereby occasioned supplied from such Class or division, by new Election, in the manner aforesaid. This Rotation shall be applied to each division, according to its number, and continued in due order annually.

The right of Suffrage in the Election of Members for both Houses shall remain as exercised at present, and each House shall choose its own Speaker, appoint its own Officers, settle its own rules of pro-ceding, and direct Writs of Election for supplying intermediate vacan-cies.

All Laws shall originate in the House of Delegates, to be approved or rejected by the Senate or to be amended with the Consent of the House of Delegates; except Money Bills, which in no instance shall be altered by the Senate but wholly approved or rejected.

A Governour, or chief Magistrate, shall be chosen annually, by joint Ballot of both Houses, (to be taken in each House respectively, de-posited in the Conference room, the Boxes examined jointly by a Committee of each House, and the numbers severally reported to them, that the appointments may be entered, which shall be the mode of taking the joint Ballot of both Houses in all Cases) who shall not continue in that office longer than three Years successively, nor be eligible until the expiration of four Years after he shall have been out of that office: An adequate, but moderate Salary, shall be settled on him during his Continuance in Office; and he shall, with the advice of a Council of State, exercise the Executive powers of Government according to the laws of this Commonwealth; and shall not, under any pretence, exercise any power or prerogative by virtue of any Law, statute, or Custom, of England; But he shall, with the advice of the Council of State, have the power of granting reprieves or pardons, except where the prosecution shall have been carried on by the House of Delegates, or the Law shall otherwise particularly direct; in which Cases, no reprieve or Pardon shall be granted but by resolve of the House of Delegates.

Either House of the General Assembly may adjourn themselves respectively: The Governour shall not prorogue or adjourn the Assembly during their setting, nor dissolve them at any Time; but he shall, if necessary, either by advice of the Council of State, or on application of a Majority of the House of Delegates, call them before the time to which they shall stand prorogued or adjourned.

A Privy Council, or Council of State, consisting of eight Members, shall be chosen by joint Ballot of both Houses of Assembly, either from their own Members or the People at large, to assist in the Administration of Government. They shall annually choose out of their own Members, a President, who, in case of the death, inability, or necessary absence of the Governour from the Government, shall act as lieutenant Governour. Four Members shall be sufficient to act, and their Advice and proceedings shall be entered of Record, and signed by the Members present (to any part whereof any Member may enter his dissent) to be laid before the General Assembly, when called for by them. This Council may appoint their own Clerk, who shall have a Salary settled by Law, and take an Oath of Secrecy in such matters as he shall be directed by the Board to conceal. A sum of Money appropriated to that purpose shall be divided annually among the Members, in proportion to their attendance; and they shall be incapable, during their continuance in Office, of sitting in either House of Assembly. Two Members shall be removed, by joint Ballot of both houses of Assembly at the end of every three Years, and be ineligible for the three next years. These Vacancies, as well as those occasioned by death or incapacity, shall be supplied by new Elections, in the same manner.

The Delegates for Virginia to the Continental Congress shall be chosen annually, or superseded in the mean time by joint Ballot of both Houses of Assembly.

The present Militia Officers shall be continued, and Vacancies supplied by appointment of the Governour, with the advice of the privy Council, or recommendations from the respective County Courts; but the Governour and Council shall have a power of suspending any Officer, and ordering a Court-Martial on Complaint for misbehaviour or inability, or to supply Vacancies of Officers happening when in actual Service. The Governour may embody the Militia, with the advice of the privy Council; and, when embodied, shall alone have the direction of the Militia under the laws of the Country.

The two Houses of Assembly shall, by joint Ballot, appoint judges of the supreme Court of Appeals, and General Court, Judges in Chancery, Judges of Admiralty, Secretary, and the Attorney-General, to be commissioned by the Governour, and continue in Office during good behaviour. In case of death, incapacity, or resignation, the Governour, with the advice of the Privy Council, shall appoint persons to succeed in office, to be approved or displaced by both Houses. These Officers shall have fixed and adequate salaries, and together with all others holding lucrative offices, and all ministers of the Gospel of every denomination, be incapable of being elected members of either House of Assembly, or the Privy Council.

The Governour, with the advice of the Privy Council, shall appoint Justices of the Peace for the counties; and in case of vacancies, or a necessity of increasing the number hereafter, such appointments to be made upon the recommendation of the respective county courts. The present acting Secretary in *Virginia,* and Clerks of all the County Courts, shall continue in Office. In case of vacancies, either by death, incapacity, or resignation, a Secretary shall be appointed as before directed, and the Clerks by the respective courts. The present and future Clerks shall hold their offices during good behaviour, to be judged of and determined in the General Court. The Sheriffs and Coroners shall be nominated by the respective courts, approved by the Governour with the advice of the Privy Council, and commissioned by the Governour. The Justices shall appoint Constables, and all fees of the aforesaid Officers be regulated by law.

The Governour, when he is out of office, and others offending against the state, either by mal-administration, corruption, or other means by which the safety of the state may be endangered, shall be impeachable by the House of Delegates. Such impeachment to be prosecuted by the Attorney-General, or such other person or persons as the House may appoint in the General Court, according to the laws of the land. If found guilty, he or they shall be either for ever disabled to hold any office under Government, or removed from such office *pro tempore,* or subjected to such pains or penalties as the laws shall direct.

If all, or any of the Judges of the General Court, should, on good grounds (to be judged of by the House of Delegates) be accused of any of the crimes or offences before-mentioned, such House of Delegates may, in like manner, impeach the Judge or Judges so accused, to be prosecuted in the Court of Appeals; and he or they, if found guilty, shall be punished in the same manner as is prescribed in the preceding clause.

Commissions and Grants shall run, *In the Name of the* COMMON-WEALTH *of* VIRGINIA, and bear teste by the Governour with the Seal of the Common wealth annexed. Writs shall run in the same manner, and bear teste by the clerks of the several courts. Indictments shall conclude, *Against the peace and dignity of the commonwealth.*

A Treasurer shall be appointed annually, by joint ballot of both Houses.

All escheats, penalties, and forfeitures, heretofore going to the King, shall go to the commonwealth, save only such, as the legislature may abolish, or otherwise provide for.

The territories contained within the Charters erecting the Colonies of *Maryland, Pennsylvania, North* and *South Carolina,* are hereby ceded, released, and forever confirmed to the people of those colonies respectively, with all the rights of property, jurisdiction, and government, and all other rights whatsoever which might at any time heretofore have been claimed by *Virginia,* except the free navigation and use of the rivers *Potowmack* and *Pohomoke,* with the property of the *Virginia* shores or strands bordering on either of the said rivers, and all improvements which have been or shall be made thereon. The western and northern extent of *Virginia* shall in all other respects stand as fixed by the charter of king James the first, in the year one thousand six hundred and nine, and by the publick treaty of peace between the courts of *Great Britain* and *France* in the year one thousand seven hundred and sixty three; unless by act of this legislature, one or more territories shall hereafter be laid off, and governments established westward of the *Allegheny* mountains. And no purchase of land shall be made of the *Indian* natives but on behalf of the publick, by authority of the General Assembly.

In order to introduce this government, the representatives of the people met in Convention shall choose a Governour and Privy Council, also such other officers directed to be chosen by both Houses as may be judged necessary to be immediately appointed. The Senate to be first chosen by the people, to continue until the last day of *March* next, and the other officers until the end of the succeeding session of Assembly. In case of Vacancies, the speaker of either House shall issue writs for new elections.

DOCUMENT No. 8

A BILL FOR ESTABLISHING RELIGIOUS FREEDOM

JANUARY 16, 1786

Well aware that the opinions and belief of men depend not on their own will, but follow involuntarily the evidence proposed to their minds; that Almighty God hath created the mind free, and manifested his supreme will that free it shall remain by making it altogether insusceptible of restraint; that all attempts to influence it by temporal punishments, or burthens, or by civil incapacitations, tend only to beget habits of hypocrisy and meanness, and are a departure from the plan of the holy author of our religion, who being lord both of body and mind, yet chose not to propagate it by coercions on either, as was in his Almighty power to do, but to extend it by its influence on reason alone; that the impious presumption of legislators and rulers, civil as well as ecclesiastical, who, being themselves but fallible and uninspired men, have assumed dominion over the faith of others, setting up their own opinions and modes of thinking as the only true and infallible, and as such endeavoring to impose them on others, hath established and maintained false religions over the greatest part of the world and through all time: That to compel a man to furnish contributions of money for the propagation of opinions which he disbelieves and abhors, is sinful and tyrannical; that even the forcing him to support this or that teacher of his own religious persuasion, is depriving him of the comfortable liberty of giving his contributions to the particular pastor whose morals he would make his pattern, and whose powers he feels most persuasive to righteousness; and is withdrawing from the ministry those temporary rewards, which proceeding from an approbation of their personal conduct, are an additional incitement to earnest and unremitting labours for the instruction of mankind; that our civil rights have no dependance on our religious opinions, any more than our opinions in physics or geometry; that therefore the proscribing any citizen as unworthy the public confidence by laying upon him an incapacity of being called to offices of trust and emolument, unless he profess or renounce this or that religious opinion, is depriving him injuriously of those privileges and advantages to which, in common with his fellow citizens, he has a natural right; that it tends also to corrupt the principles of that very religion it is meant to encourage, by bribing, with a monopoly of worldly honours and emoluments, those who will externally profess and conform to it; that though indeed these are criminal who do not withstand such temptation, yet neither are those innocent who lay the bait in their way; that the opinions of men are not the object of civil government, nor under its jurisdiction; that to suffer the civil magistrate to intrude his powers into the field of opinion and to restrain the profession or propagation of principles on supposition of their ill tendency is a dangerous falacy, which at once destroys all religious liberty, because he being of course judge of that tendency will make his opinions the rule of judgment, and approve or condemn the sentiments of others only as they shall square with or differ from his own; that it is time enough for the rightful purposes of civil government for its officers to interfere when principles break out into overt acts against peace and good order; and finally, that truth is great and will prevail if left to herself; that she is the proper and sufficient antagonist to error, and has nothing to fear from the conflict unless by human interposition disarmed of her natural weapons, free argument and debate; errors ceasing to be dangerous when it is permitted freely to contradict them.

We the General Assembly of Virginia do enact that no man shall be compelled to frequent or support any religious worship, place, or ministry whatsoever, nor shall be enforced, restrained, molested, or burthened in his body or goods, nor shall otherwise suffer, on account of his religious opinions or belief; but that all men shall be free to profess, and by argument to maintain, their opinions in matters of religion, and that the same shall in no wise diminish, enlarge, or affect their civil capacities.

And though we well know that this Assembly, elected by the people for the ordinary purposes of legislation only, have no power to restrain the acts of succeeding Assemblies, constituted with powers equal to our own, and that therefore to declare this act irrevocable would be of no effect in law; yet we are free to declare, and do declare, that the rights hereby asserted are of the natural rights of mankind, and that if any act shall be hereafter passed to repeal the present or to narrow its operation, such act will be an infringement of natural right.

Document No. 9

RESOLUTIONS FOR THE CESSION OF LANDS

JANUARY 2, 1781

In the House of Delegates
Tuesday the 2d of January 1781

The General Assembly of Virginia being well satisfied that the happiness, strength and safety of the United States depend under Providence upon the ratification of the Articles for a federal union between the United States heretofore proposed by Congress for the consideration of the said States and preferring the good of their Country to every object of smaller importance do Resolve that this Commonwealth will yeild to the Congress of the United States for the benefit of the said United States all right title and claim that the said Commonweatlh hath to the Lands Northwest of the River Ohio upon the following conditions to wit: That the territory so ceded shall be laid out and formed into States containing a suitable extent of territory and shall not be less than one hundred nor more than one hundred and fifty Miles Square, or as near thereto as circumstances will admit. That the States so formed shall be distinct republican States and be admitted Members of the federal union having the same rights of Sovereignty freedom and Independence as the other States.

That Virginia shall be allowed and fully reimbursed by the United States her actual expences in reducing the British posts at the Kaskaskies and St Vincents the expence of maintaining Garrisons and supporting civil Government there since the reduction of the said posts and in general all the charge she has incurred on Account of the Country on the Northwest side of the Ohio River since the commencement of the present War.

That the French and Canadian Inhabitants and other Settlers at the Kaskaskies St Vincents and the Neighbouring Villages who have professed themselves Citizens of Virginia shall have their possessions and titles confirmed to them and shall be protected in the enjoyment of their rights and liberty for which purpose Troops shall be stationed there at the Charge of the United States to protect them from the encroachments of the British forces at Detroit or elsewhere unless the events of War shall render it impracticable.

As Colonel George Rogers Clarke planned and executed the secret expedition by which the British posts were reduced and was promised if the enterprize succeeded a liberal gratuity in Lands in that Country for the Officers and Soldiers who first marched thither with him That a quantity of Land not exceeding one hundred and fifty thousand acres be allowed and Granted to the said officers and Soldiers and the other officers and Soldiers that have been since incorporated into the said Regiment to be laid off in one tract the length of which not to exceed double the breadth in such place on the Northwest Side of the Ohio as the majority of the officers shall choose and to be afterwards divided among the said officers and Soldiers in due proportion according to the Laws of Virginia.

That in case the quantity of good Lands of the South-East Side of the Ohio upon the Waters of Cumberland River and between the Green River and the Tenessee River which have been reserved by Law for the Virginia Troops upon Continental Establishment and upon their own State establishment should (from the North Carolina line bearing in further upon the Cumberland Lands than was expected) prove insufficient for their legal bounties the deficiency shall be made up to the said troops in good Lands to be laid off between the Rivers Scioto and little Miamis on the North-West side of the River Ohio in such proportions as have been engaged to them by the Laws of Virginia.

That all the Lands within the Territory so ceded to the United States and not reserved for or appropriated to any of the herein before mentioned purposes or disposed of in bounties to the Officers and Soldiers of the American Army shall be considered as a common Fund for the use and benefit of such of the United American States as have become or shall become Members of the confederation or federal Alliance of the said States (Virginia inclusive) according to their usual respective proportions in the general charge and expenditure and shall be faithfully and bona fide disposed of for that purpose and for no other use or purpose whatsoever. And therefore that all purchases and Deeds from any Indian or Indians or from any Indian Nation or Nations for any Lands within any part of the said territory which have been or shall be made for the use and benefit of any private person or persons whatsoever, And Royal Grants within the ceded territory inconsistent with the chartered Rights Laws and customs of Virginia, shall be deemed and declared absolutely void and of no effect in the same manner as if the said territory had still remained subject to and part of the Commonwealth of Virginia.

That all the remaining territory of Virginia included between the Atlantic Ocean and the South-East Side of the River Ohio And the

Maryland Pennsylvania and North Carolina Boundaries shall be guaranteed to the Commonwealth of Virginia by the said United States.

That the above cession of Territory by Virginia to the United States shall be void and of none effect unless all the States in the American Union shall ratify the Articles of confederation heretofore transmitted by Congress for the consideration of the said States.

Virginia having thus for the sake of the general good proposed to cede a great extent of valuable territory to the Continent, it is expected in return that every other State in the Union under similar circumstances as to vacant territory will make similar Cessions of the same to the United States for the general emolument.

Teste.

John Beckley C.H.D.

1781. Jany. 2d.
Agreed to by the Senate.
  Will Drew C.S.

Document No. 10

FORM OF RATIFICATION OF THE CONSTITUTION

JUNE 25, 1788

Virginia to wit:
We the Delegates of the People of Virginia, duly elected in pursuance of a recommendation from the General Assembly, and now met in Convention, having fully and freely investigated and discussed the proceedings of the Federal Convention and being prepared as well as the most mature deliberation hath enabled us to decide thereon Do in the name and in behalf of the People of Virginia declare and make known that the powers granted under the Constitution being derived from the People of the United States may be resumed by them whensoever the same shall be perverted to their injury or oppression, and that every power not granted thereby remains with them and at their Will: that therefore no right of any denomination can be cancelled, abridged, restrained or modified by the Congress, by the Senate or House of Representatives acting in any Capacity, by the President or any department or Officer of the United States, except in those instances in which power is given by the Constitution for those purposes: and that among other essential rights, the liberty of Conscience and of the Press cannot be cancelled, abridged, restrained, or modified by any Authority of the United States.

With these impressions, with a solemn Appeal to the Searcher of hearts for the purity of our intentions, and under the Conviction, that whatsoever imperfections may exist in the Constitution ought rather to be examined in the mode prescribed therein, than to bring the Union into danger by a delay, with a hope of obtaining Amendments previous to the Ratification.

We the said Delegates, in the name and in behalf of the People of Virginia, do by these presents assent to and ratify the Constitution recommended on the seventeenth day of September one thousand seven hundred and eighty seven by the Federal Convention for the Government of the United States; hereby announcing to all those whom it may concern, that the said Constitution is binding upon the said People, according to an authentic Copy hereto annexed in the following; . . .

Bibliographical Essay

No single work covers the history of Virginia for the whole period encompassed by this booklet. Richard L. Morton, *Colonial Virginia* (2 vols., Chapel Hill, 1960), is thorough and reliable for the period it treats, but it ends with the events of 1763. Alf J. Mapp, Jr., *The Virginia Experiment: The Old Dominion's Role in the Making of America, 1607-1781* (Richmond, 1957), written in a more popular style, stops with the battle of Yorktown. Readers might profitably consult such general works as David Hawke, *The Colonial Experience* (Indianapolis and New York, 1966), for background. This provocative and lively survey, which covers the range of American history from the era of discovery to the adoption of the federal Constitution, devotes considerable attention to events and developments in Virginia and relates them to developments in other colonies and in England.

There is also useful information in two recent histories of the state. Virginius Dabney, *Virginia: The New Dominion* (New York, 1971), is a readable survey intended for the layman; William Edwin Hemphill, Marvin Wilson Schlegel, and Sadie Ethel Engelberg, *Cavalier Commonwealth: History and Government of Virginia* (New York, 1963), is a textbook prepared for use at the senior high school level.

Several biographical works are valuable for their treatment of the revolutionary and post-revolutionary periods. Among those that deal with two or more of the documents considered here are Robert Douthat Meade's two-volume life of Patrick Henry (Philadelphia and New York, 1957-69), and the first three volumes of Irving Brant's detailed study of James Madison (6 vols., Indianapolis and New York, 1941-61). Another highly useful work is David John Mays, *Edmund Pendleton, 1721-1803: A Biography* (2 vols., Cambridge, Mass., 1952).

Extremely valuable information is found in the published writings of the Virginians of the late eighteenth century who helped to prepare most of the documents reproduced in this portfolio. In this category are *The Papers of Thomas Jefferson,* ed. Julian P. Boyd et al. (Princeton, 1950-); *The Letters and Papers of Edmund Pendleton,* ed. David John Mays (2 vols., Charlottesville, 1967); and *The Papers of George Mason, 1725-1792,* ed. Robert A. Rutland (3 vols., Chapel Hill, 1970).

The introductory essay is based largely on the texts of the documents themselves, but the author has drawn on Herbert J. Muller, *Freedom in the Western World: From the Dark Ages to the Rise of Democracy* (New York, 1963); and on Robert Allen Rutland, *The Birth of the Bill of Rights, 1776-1791* (Chapel Hill, 1955), pp. 3-23, for the origins and development of the concept of individual liberty.

Document No. 1: An Ordinance and Constitution for a Council and Assembly in Virginia, July 24, 1621.

The text of the ordinance is printed in *Records of the Virginia Company of London,* ed. Susan M. Kingsbury (4 vols., Washington, 1906-35), III, 482-84; and in Samuel M. Bemiss, ed., *The Three Charters of the Virginia Company of London* (Richmond, 1957), pp. 126-28. The history of the document and of the Virginia Company reforms of 1618 is discussed in Wesley Frank Craven, *Dissolution of the Virginia Company: The Failure of a Colonial Experiment* (New York, 1932), pp. 47-80. The same author's *Virginia Company of London, 1606-1624* (Richmond, 1957), pp. 33-34, gives a shorter account. Readers are also referred to Richard L. Morton, *Colonial Virginia,* I, 51-61; Wesley Frank Craven, *The Southern Colonies in the Seventeenth Century, 1607-1689* (Baton Rouge, 1947), pp. 125-37; Hawke, *Colonial Experience,* pp. 99-103; and Hemphill et al., *Cavalier Commonwealth,* pp. 40-42.

Document No. 2: The Declaration of the People against Sir William Berkeley, July 30, 1676.

A text of this document may be found in the *Virginia Magazine of History and Biography,* I (July, 1893), 59-61. Two full-length treatments of Bacon's Rebellion provide contrasting views of the event and of the major participants. Thomas Jefferson Wertenbaker, *Torchbearer of the Revolution: The Story of Bacon's Rebellion* (Princeton, 1940), is highly favorable to Bacon, while Wilcomb E. Washburn, *The Governor and the Rebel: A History of Bacon's Rebellion in*

Virginia (Chapel Hill, 1957), is sympathetic to Berkeley. Shorter and more balanced accounts are found in Craven, *Southern Colonies,* chapter 10; Morton, *Colonial Virginia,* I, chapters 13-15; Hawke, *Colonial Experience,* pp. 244-49; and Hemphill et al., *Cavalier Commonwealth,* pp. 61-66. The document itself is discussed by Washburn, *Governor and Rebel,* pp. 70-71, 204-05; and by Morton, *Colonial Virginia,* I, 262.

DOCUMENT NO. 3: Patrick Henry's Resolutions Against the Stamp Act, May 30, 1765.

The text of Henry's resolutions appears in Edmund S. Morgan, ed., *Prologue to Revolution: Sources and Documents on the Stamp Act Crisis, 1764-1766* (Chapel Hill, 1959), p. 48. This work also contains the text of the official version and the texts of those which appeared in the *Maryland Gazette* and the *Newport Mercury.*

The resolutions and their impact are discussed in Edmund S. Morgan and Helen M. Morgan, *The Stamp Act Crisis: Prologue to Revolution* (Chapel Hill, 1953), pp. 88-98; John Richard Alden, *The South in the Revolution, 1763-1789* (Baton Rouge, 1957), pp. 64-77; and Robert Douthat Meade, *Patrick Henry: Patriot in the Making* (Philadelphia, 1957), pp. 166-81. See also the shorter accounts in Hawke, *Colonial Experience,* pp. 535-42; and Hemphill et al., *Cavalier Commonwealth,* pp. 140-43.

DOCUMENT NO. 4: Proceedings of a Meeting of Representatives in Williamsburg, May 30, 1774.

For the text of the proceedings, see *The Papers of Thomas Jefferson,* ed. Boyd, I, 109-10. Useful accounts of this document and the events which preceded and followed its drafting are provided in Meade, *Patrick Henry: Patriot,* pp. 302-09; and David John Mays, *Edmund Pendleton,* I, 269-73. See also Hawke, *Colonial Experience,* pp. 563-69; and Hemphill et al., *Cavalier Commonwealth,* pp. 148-53.

DOCUMENT NO. 5: Resolutions of the Virginia Convention for Independence, May 15, 1776.

For the text of the resolutions, see *The Letters and Papers of Edmund Pendleton,* ed. Mays, I, 178-79; and *The Papers of Thomas Jefferson,* ed. Boyd, I, 290-91. The resolutions offered by Henry and by Meriwether Smith are in the *Virginia Magazine of History and Biography,* XVIII (January, 1910), 36-37.

Pendleton's part in the framing of the resolutions is given in Mays, *Edmund Pendleton,* II, 106-11; Henry's role is discussed in Robert

Douthat Meade, *Patrick Henry: Practical Revolutionary* (Philadelphia, 1969), pp. 102-10. Hawke, *Colonial Experience,* pp. 586-90; and Hemphill et al., *Cavalier Commonwealth,* pp. 155-56, have brief accounts of the subject.

DOCUMENT No. 6: The Virginia Declaration of Rights, June 12, 1776.
Texts of the various drafts of this document are given in *The Papers of George Mason,* ed. Rutland, I, 276-89. Rutland's editorial commentary (pp. 274-76), is highly informative, as is the analysis given by Irving Brant in *James Madison: The Virginia Revolutionist, 1751-1780* (Indianapolis, 1941), pp. 234-50. The text of the 1778 "draft" reproduced in this portfolio is in Kate Mason Rowland, *The Life of George Mason* (2 vols., New York, 1892), I, 433-36. Of this version of the declaration, Rutland has written (in *Papers of George Mason,* I, 437) that Mason "blended his memory with notes and printed texts to produce an interesting but unauthentic document."

For secondary accounts of the drafting, adoption, and influence of the Declaration of Rights, see Rutland, *The Birth of the Bill of Rights, 1776-1791,* pp. 30-40, and the same author's *George Mason: Reluctant Statesman* (New York, 1961), pp. 49-61. See also Hemphill et al., *Cavalier Commonwealth,* pp. 157-60.

DOCUMENT No. 7: A Constitution, or Form of Government, June 29, 1776.
The text of Virginia's first constitution as it was finally adopted is printed in *The Papers of George Mason,* ed. Rutland, I, 304-09, while Mason's draft may be found on pp. 299-302. Jefferson's final draft appears in *The Papers of Thomas Jefferson,* ed. Boyd, I, 356-64. See also the editorial notes by Boyd and Rutland on the development of the document in *The Papers of Thomas Jefferson,* I, 329-37; and in *The Papers of George Mason,* I, 295-99, respectively.

A long and detailed account of the writing and adoption of the constitution is in Irving Brant, *James Madison: The Virginian Revolutionist,* pp. 251-71. Briefer summaries are provided in Rutland, *George Mason: Reluctant Statesman,* pp. 61-63; and in Hemphill et al., *Cavalier Commonwealth,* pp. 158-60. For summaries of subsequent state constitutions through that of 1902, see William J. Van Schreeven, *The Conventions and Constitutions of Virginia, 1776-1966* (mimeographed, Virginia State Library, Richmond, 1967), and Hemphill et al., *Cavalier Commonwealth,* pp. 217-19, 276-79, 351-56, 412-16.

DOCUMENT NO. 8: A Bill for Establishing Religious Freedom, proposed June 12, 1779, passed January 16, 1786.

The text of Jefferson's bill appears in *The Papers of Thomas Jefferson,* ed. Boyd, II, 545-47. Boyd's editorial note on the document (pp. 547-53) is comprehensive and informative.

Dumas Malone, *Jefferson the Virginian* (Boston, 1948), pp. 274-80; and Merrill D. Peterson, *Thomas Jefferson and the New Nation: A Biography* (New York, 1970), pp. 133-45, both contain good accounts of the origins of the bill and of its final passage. Madison's role in securing its adoption is set forth in Brant, *James Madison: The Nationalist, 1780-1787* (Indianapolis, 1948), pp. 343-55; and in Adrienne Koch, *Jefferson and Madison: The Great Collaboration* (New York, 1950), pp. 26-31. Patrick Henry's role is discussed in Meade, *Patrick Henry: Practical Revolutionary,* pp. 275-81. See also Hemphill et al., *Cavalier Commonwealth,* pp. 173-75.

DOCUMENT NO. 9: Resolutions for the Cession of Lands to the United States, January 2, 1781.

The text of the resolutions is found in *The Papers of Thomas Jefferson,* ed. Boyd, IV, 386-88. Boyd's editorial note (pp. 388-90), contains much useful information. The Jones-Madison resolutions of September 6, 1780, are in *The Papers of James Madison,* ed. William T. Hutchinson et al. (Chicago, 1962-   ), II, 77-78.

The fullest account of the cession, and the circumstances that led up to it, is that given in Merrill Jensen, *The Articles of Confederation: An Interpretation of the Social-Constitutional History of the American Revolution, 1774-1781* (Madison, Wis., 1940), pp. 225-38. See also Thomas Perkins Abernethy, *Western Lands and the American Revolution* (New York, 1937; reprint, 1959), pp. 242-44, 270-73; and Alden, *South in the Revolution,* pp. 220-23. Madison's role in the matter is treated in Brant, *James Madison: The Nationalist,* pp. 89-103. See also Hawke, *Colonial Experience,* pp. 650-51, 656-61; and Hemphill et al., *Cavalier Commonwealth,* pp. 169-71.

DOCUMENT NO. 10: Form of Ratification of the Constitution, June 25, 1788.

The most available text of the ordinance is in *Documents Illustrative of the Formation of the Union of American States,* ed. Charles C. Tansill (Washington, 1927), pp. 1027-28. The amendments proposed by Virginia may be found on pp. 1028-34.

Of the various secondary accounts, that of Rutland, *Ordeal of the*

Constitution: The Antifederalists and the Ratification Struggle of 1787-1788 (Norman, Okla., 1966), chapters 10, 12, 13, is balanced and informative; also useful is Alden, *South in the Revolution,* pp. 393-98. The Virginia ratification debate is treated from the viewpoints of the major participants in such biographical works as Mays, *Pendleton,* II, chapters 14-16; Brant, *James Madison: Father of the Constitution, 1787-1800* (Indianapolis, 1950), chapters 15-17; and Meade, *Patrick Henry: Practical Revolutionary,* pp. 342-74. A brief summary is given in Hemphill et al., *Cavalier Commonwealth,* pp. 177-82.